SAVING WILD

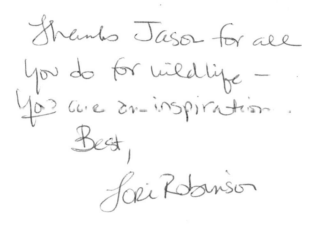

Thanks Jason for all
you do for wildlife —
You are an inspiration.
Best,
Lori Robinson

"Climate change, biodiversity loss, overexploitation — these may seem like insurmountable problems. As a lover of some of the last wilderness areas in Africa, it frightens me that they could disappear forever. Yet Lori Robinson's idea — to ask conservationists and activists how they stay inspired — should give hope and encouragement to us all. Forest ecologist Meg Lowman reminds us that "it takes the same amount of energy to complain as it does to exclaim," yet the results are so different. This book will shine a spotlight on the issues and, I hope, inspire readers to become part of the solution."

— ROXANNE REID
Author of *Travels in the Kalahari* and *A Walk in the Park*

"Thankfully, many people work hard and selflessly to protect our ecosystems, natural resources, and biodiversity. In so doing they also address poverty, hunger and thirst, thus spreading peace. It is easy to despair over what seem to be dismally stark issues; but the many threads of hope in this book are intoxicating and fortifying, thus enhancing our ability to protect this planet — since there is no Planet B."

— ALISON M. JONES
Conservation photographer and
founding director of No Water No Life, LLC

"If there is one thing I've found to be vitally important to my journey through life — it's the ability to tap into, and cultivate, inspiration. It is everything. Few people embody it as fully as Lori Robinson and the visionaries she's brought together in her brilliant book *Saving Wild*. Whether you're looking for hope in a time of great turbulence, or seeking inspiration to guide you forward, Lori knows how to find it, she knows how to live it, she knows how to bring it out in others and — most importantly, in you."

— JUSTIN FAERMAN
Co-Founder of *Conscious Lifestyle Magazine*

"It's increasingly difficult to stay inspired when the beautiful natural world that surrounds us is dwindling fast. Full of wise words from today's leading conservationists, this beautiful book makes you realize that there is still time to make a real difference. Read on and be inspired. We were."

— VICKI KENNEDY & ADAM SCOTT KENNEDY
Authors of five East Africa guide books including
Animals of the Masai Mara

SAVING WILD

Inspiration
from 50 Leading
Conservationists

Edited by LORI ROBINSON

New Insights
PRESS

Published by New Insights Press
an imprint of
Over and Above Creative Group, Los Angeles, CA
Creative Director: Susan Shankin & Associates

For permission requests, please email the publisher at following address:
rickbenzel@overandabovecreative.com.

For information, contact Over And Above Press,
8180 Manitoba Street, Unit 151, Playa del Rey, CA 90293
OverAndAboveCreative.com

First edition. Printed in the United States of America

Visit us at SavingWild.com

*For Zia, and the non-human beings and
wild places that connect us all.*

Contents

Foreword by

Jane
Goodall

THE WORLD IS IN A TRULY TERRIBLE STATE.

Species are becoming extinct. The globe is heating, ice is melting, forests are clear cut and burned, wetlands drained, oceans polluted and increasingly acidic. Above all that, we face crippling poverty on the one hand, unsustainable life styles on the other, and the sheer number of humans on the planet.

Yet I still have hope.

It is a hope that relies on conservationists, environmentalists, and humanists being able to wake up the great general public. So many people do nothing, become apathetic, because they feel helpless and hopeless. Yet billions of small ethical choices made each day will move us in the direction of a more sustainable lifestyle and help to heal the planet.

The consequences of our small choices really matter: what we buy, eat, and wear; how and where these things were made;

whether it involved cruelty to animals, slave labor, or the wasteful use of fossil fuel. Most importantly, do we NEED it? Gandhi said, so wisely, that the planet can produce enough for human need, but not for human greed. It is essential that each one of us takes action, does our bit to make this a better world.

I have other reasons for hope, like the resilience of nature, the places we despoil that, given a chance and some help, can once again support life, become safe havens for animals and plants. And the fact that animals, some on the very brink of extinction, can be given another chance. The incredible human brain has produced amazing technology that will, as it becomes mainstream, enable us to live in greater harmony with the natural world, helping each of us to choose to live in a more environmentally friendly way. The power of social media is a tool which can, for the first time in human history, rally millions of people in support of a campaign, encourage each to do his or her part, and gather in friends and acquaintances.

Finally, my hope lies in the indomitable human spirit. It's exemplified in the actions of young people who are empowered to act, once they know the problems, like the thousands involved in Roots and Shoots, my youth-led, community action program. These young people learn that each of them matters and makes a difference every day, a philosophy that remains with them as they move out into the adult world.

Most of all, that indomitable spirit is embodied in the people who tackle seemingly impossible problems, and refuse to give up, and who so often succeed — like the inspirational people in this book.

JANEGOODALL.ORG

ROOTSANDSHOOTS.ORG

INTRODUCTION

To say that this book finds its origin on the streets of London in 1934 is no exaggeration. On that April day, a new mother was discharged from a London maternity home, along with her baby girl. Deeming her husband's Aston Martin race-car too dangerous to transport their firstborn, she enlisted the help of a friend, the owner of a more sedate vehicle. It was my grandfather, Denis Robinson, who conveyed them safely home that day, an act emblematic of their friendship. But no one could have predicted that the baby clasped so carefully in her mother's arms in Grandpa's back seat, Valerie Jane Morris-Goodall, would grow up to be one of the world's most famous conservationists — and the inspiration for this book.

Jane Goodall skyrocketed to fame at 29 in the August 1963 issue of *National Geographic*, captivating readers with her feature article, "My Life Among Wild Chimpanzees." I was only a few years old at the time, but as a teenager I occasionally accompanied my grandfather to functions honoring "Dr. Jane," and like many women in my Baby Boomer generation, I idolized the courageous young British scientist living in the African bush. Later, after my grandfather died, I spent several years working as the African Adventures Specialist for the Jane Goodall Institute. It was a conversation with Dr. Jane, at one of several 80th birthday parties held in her honor, that planted the seed for *Saving Wild: Inspiration From 50 Leading Conservationists.*

ACCORDING TO SCIENTISTS, we are entering the sixth great mass extinction event, witnessing, as Jon Mooallem writes in *Wild Ones,* "a planet hemorrhaging living things so fast that half of its nine million species could be gone by the end of the century." Biological diversity is the web of life, the link uniting each organism on earth into an interdependent ecosystem in which all species have a role. Communities, families, and future generations rely on this resource. Paul Ehrlich, founder of Stanford University's Center for Conservation Biology, warns, "Such dramatic biodiversity loss will affect human health and livelihoods." Conservative estimates show that vertebrate species are disappearing faster than at any time since the extinction of the dinosaurs, threatening human existence as never before.

Changing our current environmental course is considered the greatest challenge of our time. Ehrlich adds, "Although the window of opportunity to halt, and hopefully reverse, the loss is closing, we can do it through intense conservation action." Yet thinking about the state of wildness today, it's easy to feel a sense of ecological despair, to lose hope, and to give up trying to make a difference.

It was in this pessimistic frame of mind that I arrived at Dr. Jane's birthday party. After listening to Jane give an eloquent fundraising speech, I sought her out. "How do you keep going?" I asked. "How do you stay inspired?"

A woman of consistent action and no excuses, even in her ninth decade, Dr. Jane anchored her gold-flecked eyes on mine and replied, "We can't quit. We have to keep working."

All over the world, hundreds of thousands of people and organizations are doing just that: working to halt and reverse biodiversity loss, to conserve already threatened species, to assuage the pressures from over-exploitation and climate change. But I couldn't help wondering if, like me, these people, ever get mired in the doubt and seeming impossibility of it all. And if so, how do they persevere? What is their antidote to ecological despair? Were they, like Dr. Jane, born with an unusual amount of determination, or an exceptional ability to ignore the negative? Do they possess traits that can be learned or copied?

I decided to find out.

I sought out fifty of the world's leading conservationists, men and women who have devoted their lives to saving some of the most endangered species and the most threatened areas on earth. Among the people I contacted were wildlife filmmakers Beverly and Dereck Joubert, elephant experts Daphne Sheldrick, Cynthia Moss and Joyce Poole, and ocean warrior Paul Watson. I spoke with Boyd Varty, who was raised in the African bush, with Kristine McDivitt Tompkins, former CEO of Patagonia, and with Laura Turner, daughter of one of America's most prominent conservationists. To each, I posed the question I had asked Jane: How do you stay inspired? I wanted to know how, involved in what tree ecologist Meg Lowman says is probably one of "the most depressing fields of work on the planet right now," these people create enough reserves of hope and inspiration to overcome the worst moments of despair.

The answers I received are more personal, heartfelt, and inspiring than I could have imagined. "The biggest threats . . . can feel totally insurmountable," admits Saba Douglas-Hamilton, director of Elephant Watch Portfolio. "But . . . we are living in an age of transformation. The social networks that encircle the globe are tentacles of consciousness, acting as lightening conductors for common outrage about environmental crime, while green technologies are giving us a glimpse of a world beyond fossil fuels that is now truly within our reach."

Not only optimism, but a contagious determination permeates the responses. As author Tina Welling reminds us, "We are amazing beings. We can accomplish anything we give our attention to." That is the gift of the people in this book. Their determination lifts and holds me up, motivating me to keep trying. I hope their voices will inspire everyone who cares about the state of our planet today.

Many of the conservationists featured in this book find motivation in the resilience of nature itself. Marine ecologist Alasdair Harris takes heart in "observing nature's incredible ability to regenerate and bounce back. Whether it's the way life and abundance return in spring, or the way wilderness recovers in a protected area, the unstoppable resilience of nature on the rebound is a source of great hope." Others are driven by a sense of urgency, and many share Ted Turner's conviction that they have no choice but to keep trying. In Todd Wilkinson's book about Turner, *The Last Stand*, the CNN founder quotes his mentor, ocean protector extraordinaire, Jacque Cousteau: "What can men of good conscience do but keep trying to do the right thing until the very end?"

When we work together to do the right thing, the effectiveness of our individual efforts is exponentially enhanced.

Climate change expert Naomi Klein, author of *This Changes Everything*, understands that collective power. At an event I attended she told the audience, "I am part of this amazing growing movement, and that keeps me optimistic. If I ever imagined that this was a campaign about me against the world, I would be desperately depressed."

Several *Saving Wild* contributors express similar sentiments, citing as inspiration all the people they meet who are doing amazing work on behalf of the planet. One of these conservationists, videographer Bill Wallauer, offers practical advice for anyone overwhelmed by despair about the state of our world: "Join a group of determined people who have changed policy, cleaned up their neighborhoods, saved a species from extinction," he urges. I can think of no more determined group than the extraordinary individuals in this book. It's my hope that their enthusiasm and dedication will inspire each one of us to work harder at saving the wildlife and wild places that connect us all. And then let's take Jane's advice: "Don't give up."

PIONEERS

---

*The conservationists in this group have spent
the majority of their lives working to preserve wildlife and
wild places, and are pioneers in their field They enjoy
worldwide name recognition, have won numerous awards,
and are often cited as mentors by conservationists in the
generations that followed them.*

Beverly & Dereck Joubert

Co-Founders, Great Plains Foundation, Botswana

Dereck and Beverly Joubert are award-winning film-makers and are National Geographic Explorers-in-Residence based in Botswana. Their mission is the conservation and understanding of the large predators and key African wildlife species that determine the course of all conservation in Africa. Their coverage of unique predator behavior over the past 25 years has resulted in 22 films, ten books, six scientific papers, and many articles for *National Geographic* magazine. They have won five Emmys, a Peabody, the World Ecology Award, and were recently inducted into the American Academy of Achievement.

How We Stay Inspired

⁂

DISCOVERING GREAT INDIVIDUAL CHARACTERS, like the little leopard that we followed for over five years for our wildlife film *Eye of the Leopard,* certainly inspires us to speak out and be their voices, and it keeps us focused on the reasons why we need to protect their wilderness. If we can tell their amazing stories in an intimate and personal way, we know they will be given a chance. These special characters also often become the best ambassadors for their species, as they touch people around the world and hopefully make them care and want to help protect these amazing creatures.

Over the past 50 years we have lost between 90-95% of Africa's large predators. Large predators have gone extinct in 26 African countries already. We have become ambassadors for these animals out of necessity and feel we must protect the last remaining ones in the few countries where they still exist. The urgency of the situation and knowing all that could be lost keeps us going. Time is running out for our remaining wild places and the animals that depend on them, due to ever-increasing poaching. This is our driving force, and through our films and my photography we can keep attention on the problems and causes by speaking out for them.

If we focus only on the sacrifices we have made, then life will certainly become unpleasant and unrewarding. So there is another way of looking at those sacrifices . . . they have turned us into who we are today, advocates and ambassadors for the African wilderness and its wildlife (particularly big cats, as by protecting them we in turn protect every other animal). Every sacrifice can be seen as a gain; it's just about always seeing the positive in whatever life hands you, and doing the best you can with it, to achieve all that you can be for yourself and the world around you.

GREATPLAINSFOUNDATION.COM

Paul
Watson

Founder, Sea Shepherd Conservation Society, France

Canadian Captain Paul Watson is the co-founder of the Greenpeace Foundation (1972), founder of the Sea Shepherd Conservation Society (1977), and was the national director of the Sierra Club from 2003 to 2006. He was awarded the Amazon Peace Prize in 2007 by the president of Ecuador and the Jules Verne Award for environment activism in 2012. He is the author of the books *Ocean Warrior, Seal Wars* and *Earthforce!*

How I Stay Inspired

FIVE REASONS.

First, because I am fortunate in not having to deal with stress in my life. I do what I can do and I do not stress about consequences outside of my control.

Second, because I live my life in accordance with the laws of ecology, and I view life from a bio-centric perspective. What this means is that I have faith that the earth will protect itself from us, because no species can survive outside of the boundaries of the laws of diversity, interdependence, and finite resources. I aspire to do what I can to help mitigate the consequences, both for other species and ourselves.

Third, I believe that the solution to an impossible situation is an impossible answer, and I believe that the impossible can be made possible. For example, in 1972 the very idea that Nelson Mandela would be president of South Africa was unthinkable and impossible, yet it became possible.

Fourth, because I believe in the power of individual will, and I believe that a small group of people can change the world through the harnessing of their imagination and passion, and their skills of courage, determination and patience.

Finally, by experiencing nature on the water, under the sea, in the forests, and on the plains. And acknowledgement of the importance of all other species, and understanding that our future depends upon ensuring their future, and that if the ocean and the forests die, we all die!

SEASHEPHERDGLOBAL.COM

Paul R. Ehrlich

Bing Professor of Population Studies
President, Center for Conservation Biology,
Stanford University, USA

Paul R. Ehrlich has been a household name since the publication of his 1968 bestseller, *The Population Bomb*. He is a member of the National Academy of Sciences and a recipient of the Crafoord Prize, the Blue Planet Prize, and numerous other international honors. He investigates a wide range of topics in population biology, ecology, evolution, and human ecology and evolution. Much of his current effort is focused on the mechanisms of human cultural evolution and on ways of directing that evolution to ameliorate the human predicament.

How I Stay Inspired

I GET AND MAINTAIN my inspiration from two basic sources. The first is children: Anne's and my daughter, grandchildren, and great grandchildren, and the wonderful offspring of friends and colleagues. They are all bright, lucky (compared to kids I've known in poor countries), and mostly ignorant of the disaster toward which humanity is heading. I can't just do nothing and enjoy the end of my life, knowing that young people are unlikely to be able to have anything like my opportunities, just as it's been difficult throughout my life to enjoy things I've known are not available to billions of other people. I have a difference with a valued colleague, Jim Brown, the world's top bio geographer. I think there's about a 10% chance to avoid a collapse of civilization; Jim thinks it's only about 1% (and in response to the political situation, I'm beginning to think Jim is right!). But we agree that it's worth it for me to work hard to increase the chances of civilization persisting to 10.1%, and for him to struggle to make it 1.1%. We'll go down fighting for a sustainable civilization, and the "we"

is a loving wife and a mob of great colleagues and friends —
a "band of brothers."

The other source of inspiration for me is the beauty, intricacy, and interest of the animals and plants of our planet. They are our only known living companions in the universe — and we're wiping them out. Anne and I and our close colleague Gerardo Ceballos used this inspiration to produce a beautifully illustrated book, *The Annihilation of Nature*, to introduce people to the birds and mammals that are disappearing and to raise funds to support the training of young conservation scientists. Some of the happiest times of my life have been spent with non-humans, diving on the great barrier reef, gathering data on the behavior of gorgeous butterfly fishes, watching aardvarks forage in the South African night, seeing a pair of endangered golden-shouldered parrots return to the nest they had bored in a termite nest after waiting for several hours in northeastern Australia, or discovering that patterns on many butterfly wings appear to be representations of caterpillars. Appreciation and discovery inspire me to keep doing all I can to preserve biodiversity, and thus our life-support systems. It's a fun crusade.

CCB.STANFORD.EDU/PAUL-R-EHRLICH

Iain Douglas-Hamilton

Founder, Save The Elephants, Kenya

Iain Douglas-Hamilton was the first to alert the world to the ivory poaching holocaust, and he helped bring about the world ivory trade ban in 1989. In 1993 he founded Save the Elephants, nurturing a new generation of wildlife researchers and conservationists in Kenya and around the world. In Africa, Douglas-Hamilton pioneered GPS tracking of elephants, which has become a standard and widely emulated survey technique. His 2013 meeting at the White House was followed by President Obama's Executive Order to stop the poaching of elephants and rhinos, as well as by a Commitment to Action from the Clinton Global Initiative, supporting governments in anti-poaching and trafficking efforts. Currently Douglas-Hamilton is focused on winning hearts and minds in China to help reduce the demand for ivory driving the illegal killing of elephants.

How I Stay Inspired

WHENEVER I FEEL DOWN I go and hang out with the elephants in Samburu, who are very used to me and allow me into their world to watch as a silent observer. I see the young mothers who have grown up from childhood, and I get my elephant fix for a few hours. This re-invigorates me to face and combat the awful realities of the elephants' situation in Africa today.

Elephant populations across Africa have been falling like dominoes. The once-widespread elephants disappeared into tiny, isolated pockets long ago. It took years for scientists to penetrate the forests and accumulate reliable facts on elusive forest elephants that inhabit them. Technology has made the fight to protect these magnificent species a real inspiration. With the pioneering of the GPS tracking system, this has enabled the protection of key elephant populations while further helping in anti-poaching efforts.

Over the past few years, wildlife trafficking has become more organized, more lucrative, more widespread, and more dangerous than ever before. The ivory trade is the greatest threat to elephants, one that threatens to wipe them from the wilds of Africa. Behind the many facets of the current crisis is the swelling demand for ivory. The race is on to convince China's affluent middle class of the terrible impacts of buying ivory, before elephants succumb to the unbridled desire for their tusks. Various collaborations of concerned individuals, non-governmental organizations (NGOs), institutions and governments playing such a big role in demand reduction gives me such joy and hope that we are all working together to ensure the survival of elephants.

SAVETHEELEPHANTS.ORG

Daphne Sheldrick

Founder, David Sheldrick Wildlife Trust, Kenya

Daphne Sheldrick is considered the world's expert in raising orphaned elephants. She founded the David Sheldrick Wildlife Trust and its pioneering Orphans Project, both global forces for wildlife conservation. Her work has been honored by the government of Kenya and the British Broadcasting Company. In the 2006 New Year's Honors List, Queen Elizabeth II appointed Dr. Daphne Sheldrick to Dame Commander of the Most Excellent Order of the British Empire, the first knighthood to be awarded in Kenya since the country gained independence in 1963. Her extraordinary life is captured in her memoir *Love, Life and Elephants*.

How I Stay Inspired

Life is never a bed of roses. By involving oneself in the natural world, one understands that the other beings that share our planet home have to cope with far worse traumas, and yet find the courage to turn the page and focus on the living.

The elephants in particular have given me the strength to emulate them in this way. There are always highs and lows in the work I do, but one simply has to cope and accept the rough with the smooth!

There is enormous benefit for those that study and love the natural world and its wild inhabitants, irrespective of species. It gives one inspiration. One is never bored, lonely, or living in isolation, and there are lessons to learn from nature that stand you in good stead. It takes sincere empathy, compassion, understanding, and above all, passion and perseverance.

Thousands of African children (and other people) have come to view the orphaned elephants daily at my home when the animals come to the compound to take their noon milk feed and enjoy a mud bath. We open our doors to the public for one hour, and to those that have supported the orphans through our online digital fostering program every day from 5 – 7 p.m., to see the orphans being put in their stockades and stables for the night, and to be able to speak to the keepers who replace their lost elephant families. Through the monthly Keepers' Diaries on the Internet, millions of people worldwide have learnt about the nature of these highly sophisticated and intelligent animals that mirror us emotionally — are just like us, but better than us in many ways. My autobiography has been translated into most foreign languages, including Mandarin. In that way we have done all we can to inspire others to be caring of the Natural World. And this in turn keeps me inspired.

SHELDRICKWILDLIFETRUST.ORG

Lori Robinson 17

Cynthia Moss

Director, Amboseli Trust For Elephants, Kenya

Born and educated in the U.S.A., Cynthia Moss moved to Africa in 1968 and has spent the past 47 years there studying elephants and working for their conservation. In 1972 she started the Amboseli Elephant Research Project (AERP) in Kenya. Her present activities include directing and supervising research, disseminating scientific results, and promoting public awareness about elephants. Moss has written numerous books and popular and scientific articles, and she has made six award-winning television documentaries about elephants. In 2002 she was awarded a MacArthur "genius" fellowship.

How I Stay Inspired

IT'S NOT DIFFICULT TO stay inspired when one is dealing with elephants. They are infinitely inspirational—long-lived, intelligent, intensely social, charismatic, empathetic, amusing, endearing and more. Anyone could be inspired by elephants without ever seeing them in the wild.

For me, knowing individual elephants has been the key to my passion and commitment. Once I could recognize individuals and I had named them, I felt a responsibility for each of those elephants lives. It was something like a pact: you allow me to study you, to sit quietly with you and record your behavior, and, most significant, you trust me; in turn I will do everything in my power to keep you safe from harassment, from fear, from pain, and from a violent death.

Of course, there are bad days when it seems impossible to conserve elephants, but I have never once thought of giving up. How could I walk away from Enid and Eliot, Jolene and Jamila, Tim and Tolstoy and the rest of the Amboseli elephants and all those across Africa and Asia?

There is nothing heroic or commendable about my position, there is simply no choice for me.

ELEPHANTTRUST.ORG

Ian
Player

Founder, Wilderness Leadership School, South Africa

Ian Player is often referred to as South Africa's father of conservation. Dr. Player helped start the first protected status for parks in South Africa and worked to save that country's rhinos from extinction. Founder of The WILD Foundation, the World Wilderness Congress and the Wilderness Leadership School, his insistence that matters of spirit were as important to conservation as science, and that people and cultures are an important part of the environmental equation, revolutionized conservation efforts worldwide.

How I Stay Inspired

THE POSITIVE RESPONSES I have witnessed from those who have experienced the wilderness long ago made me realize how important being in the wilderness is to spiritual development of the individual. My Zulu companion and mentor, Magqubu Ntombela, always used to say that the work we were doing to protect wildlife and wild places was for God, and if God was with us, as he believed being a Shembe, we just had to keep going.

In 1955 I faced a crisis while fighting for the game reserves in Zululand because some of my colleagues were very depressed and thought we stood no chance. It was my experiences in the wilderness on my river journeys in a canoe when, at times, everything seemed hopeless, that inspired me and convinced me never to give up.

NOTE: Dr. Ian Player passed away a few months after he was interviewed for this book.

WILD.ORG

INFLUENCERS

---

*The role of non-governmental organizations (NGOs)
as powerful forces in conservation, especially in
those areas where government bodies have failed or
responded inadequately, is acknowledged worldwide.
The conservationists in this group wield their extensive
influence as presidents, consultants, board members,
and regional and/or species specific directors for some of
the most effective NGOs on the planet.*

Azzedine
Downes

President, International Fund For Animal Welfare, USA

Azzedine T. Downes is the president and CEO of U.S. based International Fund for Animal Welfare, a conservation organization with projects in forty countries around the world. He is an advisor to the Global Tiger Forum and to the Obama Administration on illegal wildlife trade protections, as well as a member of the Clinton Global Initiative Elephant Task Force. He holds a masters degree from Harvard University in planning and social policy and speaks English, Arabic and French.

How I Stay Inspired

IN A WORLD WHERE headlines on all topics are most likely depressing, it is a challenge to remain positive in conservation when we are surrounded by so much bad news daily. My experience has been that people working in conservation divide themselves into two broad categories: those fighting against something and those fighting for something. I find that those who describe themselves as fighting against what is happening to wildlife and their habitats often withdraw from the very interactions that are most critical to change, namely changing human behavior. They are often consumed and paralyzed by the sheer horror of the possibility of extinction and environmental catastrophe.

I include myself in the category of people who describe themselves as fighting for something and that is how I remain inspired. I also believe in taking a holistic view of the problem and look to identify the most fundamental questions upon which people can agree. I recently listened to Sir Richard Branson speak in New York, and he told us about the observations of astronauts looking down on the earth and coming to the conclusion that strife between nations is never justified; a planetary view, to be sure. I first seek to obtain agreement that people will make a commitment to coexist with other animals on the planet. There are a million ways to achieve that goal, but without agreement on the goal, destruction of the planet and its wildlife will continue.

We, as a species, can choose to evolve and we must if we are to save the planet and its wildlife. I remain inspired because of the people I meet around the world who choose, at a minimum, to coexist with wildlife even in the face of personal sacrifice. I am further inspired by the people who believe that individual animals matter, individual lives matter, and who reject the notion that simply stockpiling an ample number of animals around the world defines conservation.

IFAW.ORG

Laura Turner Seydel

Chairperson, Captain Planet Foundation, USA

Laura Turner Seydel is an international environmental advocate and eco-living expert dedicated to creating a healthy and sustainable future for our children. She is chairperson of the Captain Planet Foundation, which funds environmental stewardship projects worldwide. She co-founded Mothers and Others for Clean Air and Chattahoochee Riverkeeper. She serves on the board of directors for The Turner Foundation, the Environmental Working Group, the League of Conservation Voters, Defenders of Wildlife, Waterkeeper Alliance, the Carter Center Board of Councilors, the Rotary Club of Downtown Atlanta and on the advisory board for the Ray C. Anderson Foundation. Turner Seydel lives with her husband and her three children in the first LEED certified Gold residence in the southeastern U.S.

How I Stay Inspired

"We do not inherit the Earth from our ancestors, we borrow it from our children." —*Native American Proverb*

THERE ARE THREE THINGS that give me hope as the sixth mass extinction progresses at a rapid pace. The first is a great film called *Racing Extinction*, by Academy Award-winning director Louis Psihoyos, that makes a compelling case for the actions humanity can take to change things for the better and why we have to act urgently. After the film's theatrical release, the Discovery Channel broadcasted *Racing Extinction* globally before the Paris climate negotiations in December 2015. They estimated that one billion people saw the film!

In addition, I am hopeful that Pope Francis' momentous first-ever address to the U.S. Congress and UN General Assembly will make a real difference. Pope Francis made it clear that humans are not fulfilling our role as stewards of God's creation, and that we are abusing and destroying nature and the planet's life support system for profit. Leader of the world's

1.2 billion Catholics, Pope Francis has two billion followers on Facebook and is effectively using social media to spread his message and his calls for us to act. I believe in divine intervention and I believe if we are mindful and prayerful about our responsibility the path to success will become clearer.

And last, what gives me hope, and serves as my primary motivation, are the children who expect us to be responsible and make sure their future is bright so that they can live and thrive. More and more, I see mindsets changing. I was recently at the UN, where the General Assembly launched the 17 Sustainable Development Goals (SDGs). The SDGs are the first holistic global plan, two years in the making, in which experts from the global north and south have come together to see how we can achieve healthcare, education, and clean, affordable energy for all, while at the same time saving the natural systems that support all life.

All of these things give me hope, and it's essential for us to focus on ecosystem restoration and to use everything in our toolbox to do so as quickly as possible. This goal is easier to achieve if we keep in mind that there is no healthy economy without healthy, functioning ecosystem services.

CAPTAINPLANETFOUNDATION.ORG

LAURASEYDEL.COM

Gloria Flora

Executive Director, Sustainable Obtainable Solutions, USA

Named one of the most influential environmentalists by Time Magazine, Gloria Flora served 23 years in the U.S. Forest Service working in a variety of positions, including as the Forest Supervisor on the largest national forest in the continental U.S. She is the founder and executive director of Sustainable Obtainable Solutions, whose focus is on large landscape conservation strategies, national and international climate change action planning, and promoting the sustainable production and use of biochar. Flora has won multiple awards for her leadership, courage and environmental stewardship, including having a new species of Tanzanian toad named after her.

How I Stay Inspired

EVERY TIME I DRAFTED something to answer this question, I ended up with hollow platitudes that even I couldn't swallow. True, there are wonderful people doing wonderful things, and nature continues to inspire in its intricacy, stunning beauty and relationships. Even a handful of soil is more complex than me. But the plain truth is that I'm not inspired these days. The more I know, the more I despair.

I realize, despite the beating we've given it, there are parts of the planet that may soldier on. However, there are many tragedies of plants, animals and humans unfolding, and more coming. I continue to work even harder and longer than I ever have, driving myself almost to distraction in my efforts. Not because I'm inspired, but because I have three grandchildren, and I'm desperate.

Sure, we have some victories. But in the big picture we have not yet reached one degree Celsius in increase in world temperature warming, and it's clear that even that is bringing about a chain reaction of events, throwing species, landscapes and people into decline on every continent. We'd like to think that if we can hold it at a gain of two degrees Celsius, we can regain some equilibrium. That would be geometrically increasing the kind of perturbations we see now. The 2105 Paris Conference of Parties acknowledged the need to phase out fossil fuels but proffered only a tenuous promise of voluntary acts. Unfulfilled, that's a death sentence to the planet. Again, I am not inspired, I'm desperate.

I wrote this for *The Global Chorus: 365 Voices on the Future of the Planet*: The eye of the needle seems to be shrinking. I plant trees, I grow food, I tend animals, I do permaculture design, fight for precious landscapes, collaborate to restore forests, teach people about biochar and its climate and soil wonders and work unceasingly to make our descent, and that of all living beings, more gentle and humane. But to say I'm inspired is just not true.

S-O-SOLUTIONS.ORG

Ian Redmond

Ambassador, Unep Convention On Migratory Species, UK

A naturalist by birth, and a biologist by training, U.K. based Ian Redmond is a conservationist by necessity, focused on saving wild gorillas. Best known for his work studying the mountain gorillas of Rwanda with zoologist Dian Fossey, who inspired the film *Gorillas in the Mist*, Redmond has dedicated his life to raising awareness of the great apes' plight, kick-starting a UN initiative in 2000, GRASP (Great Apes Survival Partnership), dedicated to the species he knows best.

How I Stay Inspired

THE PERSONAL PAY-OFF FROM my work is that I spend time in nature (whether in the UK or around the world). Animal behavior fascinates me, as does communication — verbal and non-verbal. I find there is a real thrill when connecting with another being (human or non-human), whether that is by grooming an individual primate, blowing gently down an elephant's trunk or speaking to an audience of thousands.

I'm one of those infuriatingly cheerful chaps whatever the weather, and despite on rare occasions witnessing the worst that humans can do–both to themselves and to other species — I am also greatly encouraged by the acts of kindness and bravery I have seen in the most dire circumstances. An elephant matriarch guiding a baby to safety with her trunk; gorilla parents protecting their infant, each in turn protected by courageous rangers; a mother's love for her child — expressed through gesture or simple eye contact. All of these things keep me inspired.

4APES.COM

Saba Douglas-Hamilton

Director, Elephant Watch Portfolio, Kenya

Saba Douglas-Hamilton is a Kenyan conservationist, communicator and television host. She joined Save the Elephants (STE) as head of operations in 1997, served as a trustee for a decade and is now chair of the advisory board. In 2000 she began her career as a wildlife filmmaker, hosting nine television series including *Secret Life of Elephants*, *Big Cat Diary*, and *Unknown Africa*, and over twenty-four documentaries for the BBC, as well as producing two award-winning films for Animal Planet, *Heart of a Lioness* and *Rhino Nights*. Her newest film is a 12-part BBC series, *This Wild Life*. She runs her family's eco-lodge, Elephant Watch Camp, in Samburu.

How I Stay Inspired

WILD SPACES ARE MY cathedral, the place I go to lose myself in wonder at the infinite variety of the natural world. I am continually awed by the beauty of the biosphere, by life crafted over billions of years and the interconnectivity of all living things. For me, nothing else inspires greater reverence nor provides greater inspiration. This is where I find my strength.

The torrent of reports we receive on a daily basis, detailing the insults and injuries humanity is inflicting on nature, blacken the soul, and the biggest threats—climate change, ocean acidification, human population growth, wildlife trafficking— can feel totally insurmountable. But there are glimmers of hope, for we are living in an age of transformation. The social networks that encircle the globe are tentacles of consciousness, acting as lightening conductors for common outrage about environmental crime, while green technologies are giving us a glimpse of a world beyond fossil fuels that is now truly within our reach.

While the big issues need all of us to be informed and involved, most of the time all one can influence are the things in one's immediate vicinity. In Samburu we're blessed to be working with amazing people from the local nomadic communities, who are helping create real solutions, and that's something that gives me hope on a daily basis. So do the eco-warriors fighting on the front line, be they rangers or activists, lawyers or filmmakers. I'm inspired by the capacity of wild species to re-seed themselves and of nature to re-wild, given the chance. Humanity is certainly nature's biggest problem, but I have great faith in the power of human sentiment. When you love something, you fight to protect it. So we need to talk more about reverence for nature and compassion for other living creatures and keep spreading the word. More than anything, I see hope because of my children–in their love of wild things and wilderness. I will do everything in my power to ensure that they have a sustainable future.

ELEPHANTWATCHPORTFOLIO.COM

Annette Lanjouw

VP, Strategic Initiatives and Great Ape Program,
Arcus Foundation, UK

Annette Lanjouw joined the U.K. based Arcus Foundation in 2007 and now leads their work of ensuring the respect and survival of great apes and their natural habitat across their range. She has worked across Central Africa on the conservation and research of bonobos, chimpanzees and mountain gorillas, and she brings experience in the areas of behavioral ecology, conservation strategy, organizational management, institutional development and policy to her work across Africa and Southeast Asia.

How I Stay Inspired

THERE ARE COUNTLESS CHALLENGES that can make conservation of wildlife and protecting landscapes and environments from destruction seem almost overwhelmingly difficult...and perhaps even sometimes impossible. And yet, I know very few conservationists who give up. I do know that cynicism is a mentality that can creep in to some people's minds, yet even that is relatively rare, and extremely unproductive. We stay inspired because there are numerous sources of inspiration, despite the overwhelming challenges.

Firstly, the animals themselves and the incredible places of wilderness in the world remain an eternal source of inspiration. They are beautiful, sentient and fascinating, and they need the help of people who understand that the world can only survive if it is diverse and there is space for all the creatures and varied ecosystems to continue to exist. Deliberate conservation efforts are necessary because the paradigm of consumption and economic growth leads to unsustainable exploitation and destruction without measures for protection.

Secondly, the people who are committed to and engaged in conservation are not just a handful of eccentrics but people of all nationalities, all levels of education, all cultures and religions. This incredible cohort of intelligent, dedicated and often unbelievably brave individuals is a true community and movement of people that represent the diversity of humanity in all its most wonderful forms. This community shows me that the conservation movement is grounded in all of humanity across the globe and will eventually result in success.

ARCUSFOUNDATION.ORG

Boyd Varty

World Village Builder, Londolozi Nature Reserve, South Africa

Growing up surrounded by lions, leopards, snakes and elephants on his family's South African nature preserve, "Londolozi," Zulu for "protector of all living things, Boyd Varty's life has been, and will continue to be, formed by that ideal. Today he continues his mission of linking the growth of the human mind and spirit with the restoration of ecosystems. In 2014 Varty published his memoir, *Cathedral of the Wild*. As a coach, he introduces first-world seekers to an intimate relationship with the wild, and he devotes himself to healing not only landscapes and animals, but the people and human systems that must coexist with nature to create a healthy and sustainable future for life.

How I Stay Inspired

I KEEP MYSELF INSPIRED by making sure I keep perspective.

We are not destroying the natural world . . . we are destroying ourselves. Mother Nature is ancient and timeless. It is said that it would take no more than 100 years for the earth to restore itself to perfect balance if humans all died out. So I maintain that macro view, and it gives me hope on a grand scale.

Then, on a day-to-day basis, I return to my own enchantment with the natural world and let that be a driving inspiration. Every tree is a poem to being, every animal a friend to the spirit. Every day amidst all the chaos and destruction I find a small moment in nature to keep my heart full of the desire to be a part of a growing tribe of people who are trying to create a new consciousness that will be the catalyst for global change.

BOYDVARTY.COM

Braam Malherbe

Extreme Conservationist, South Africa

Braam Malherbe is a South African based international motivational speaker, an extreme adventurer, television presenter and author; but most of all he is a no-nonsense conservationist. Using his unbridled passion for the natural world, Malherbe inspires people to be part of the change required for a sustainable future for all species on the planet. His extreme adventures include running the entire length of the Great Wall of China in a single attempt, and alongside Pete van Kets he will circumnavigate (with zero carbon emissions) the Tropic of Capricorn. As an honorary ranger for SANParks, Malherbe was involved in anti-poaching operations to save the rhino from extinction. He is spearheading a Do One Thing (DOT) movement for the planet using a free mobile app as a vehicle for change.

How I Stay Inspired

SPECIES HAVE BEEN EVOLVING on earth for approximately 3.4 billion years. We humans have been here for a nanosecond, and in this short time we have been responsible for possibly the greatest extinction in earth's history. How then does one remain inspired with such tragedy happening daily? Nature is profound in its many simple lessons. There are two lessons I resonate strongly with. The first is that in natural systems, if you are not an asset you are a liability. Take for example an injured or weak animal. It does not last long. The second lesson is that every species fights for survival, but it does not destroy all the food resources of other species. The zebra and wildebeest do not eat all of the grass; the lion does not kill all of the impala. We are the only species that destroy all species to grow one crop for one species. We will move rocks, destroy trees, plough the land and plant a single crop. We will decimate the land for our own selfish needs alone, totally disrespecting the rights of other species.

So how do I remain positive and inspired when I live in a world of over-consumption and greed? We are meant to be custodians of the earth, not pillagers. This is what drives me: to be an asset to this, our Earth, our only home. We are known as the 'lucky planet.' If we were just a small distance closer to the sun, we would have no water. If we were a little further away, we would be frozen solid. Indeed, if we were not tilted on our axis, we would not have seasons as we know them, and therefore not have the incredible biodiversity of life. It is nature that restores my soul. Nature that gives me hope. The wilderness that speaks volumes to me in its silence.

The word "crisis" in Mandarin is made of two words: the cri, loosely interpreted, means "fear" or "danger." The sis means "opportunity." This is indeed how it is. We humans tend to change for one of two reasons; we are forced to, or we rise to a higher level of respect and reverence for all life. Both are happening in my lifetime. We are stressing ecosystems, and in turn, we are being forced to change. Also, I see change in our youth, a deeper respect for our wild places and a shift from only material gain to one of personal significance. This gives me great hope!

I am gifted to be able to speak to large audiences all over the world about my expeditions and what they have taught me. I am grateful for this gift and impart my sharing with humility. My speeches are a constant motivation to me as well as my audiences.

BRAAMMALHERBE.COM

Suzanne Stone

Wolf Specialist, Defenders Of Wildlife, USA

Suzanne Asha Stone has worked in wolf restoration in the northern Rockies since 1988, including serving as a member of the 1995/1996 USA/Canadian wolf reintroduction team. She currently oversees Defenders Of Wildlife programs for wolf conservation and restoration in Idaho, Montana, Oregon, Washington, and Wyoming.

How I Stay Inspired

❦

WORKING FOR WOLVES IS truly a lifelong calling, not just a job, so I'm inspired by my passion for the species. However, wolf work is among the most brutal in terms of the hostility toward the species. Wolves have long been persecuted, but the conflicts today have created deeply polarized divisions that thrust wolf conservationists into the line of fire in efforts to protect wolves. I've been on the front line of this battle for nearly 30 years. Staying inspired despite the widespread killing of wolves, despite the continued prejudice and ignorance that shrouds their survival, despite the lack of compassion toward even their young, is one of the toughest challenges I've ever faced.

The only way to stay inspired is to stay connected to nature. I grow my own food and regularly exercise outdoors. I camp in the backcountry when possible, long enough to release the mind chatter and embrace the silence. When things get severe, I camp alone for days to ground myself and release stress. I enjoy music — singing and drumming — and reading and other forms of art. Keeping a strong connection to Source of Life energy in all its forms can help maintain inspiration. Also, training others to do the same work helps reduce the burden of my work by sharing the load. I journal and reflect when I feel overwhelmed or under-appreciated. I spend time with animals and children. Both help remind me that our work is for the voiceless, and without us, they have no protection. This is not a job. It is a calling. And if all else fails, I re-read *Thinking Like A Mountain* by Aldo Leopold, and it restores my faith that it is all worth the effort.

DEFENDERS.ORG/STAFF/SUZANNE-ASHA-STONE

Alison Holloran

Executive Director, Audubon Rockies
VP, National Audubon Society, USA

Alison Holloran holds a BS in wildlife management from the University of West Virginia and a MS in zoology and physiology from the University of Wyoming. She served two years with the United States Peace Corps as a wildlands promoter in Honduras, and she worked for the Wyoming Cooperative Fish and Wildlife Research Unit developing and executing a research plan examining the potential effects of natural gas development on sage-grouse populations. Holloran has been with the Audubon Society for 14 years.

How I Stay Inspired

THE CONSERVATION OF OUR wild lands and wildlife has been a lifelong commitment of mine. Growing up, as far back as I can remember, when asked, "What do you want to be when you grow up?" I had the same answer: "Wildlife Biologist," of course! Over the course of many years plans change, but I have stuck to my word. As the executive director of Audubon Rockies, I face many ups and downs every day. And to be clear, I do get discouraged, frustrated, and just down right disheartened. So what keeps me inspired? I suppose I could say hiking, being out of doors, etc. although I think of them as affirmations, not inspirations. Despite inevitable failures and disappointments there are three factors that I fall back on every day, that remind me of how I can, should, and will move forward. The first reminder and inspiration are my two beautiful girls, Sage and Willow. I look at them every day, hear them talk to me about their hopes for the day, year, their lives, and think, "I owe this to them." I brought them into this world, this was my choice, and so for their health, dreams, and opportunities I owe them a healthy environment, a place where they can observe the wonder of the natural world and marvel at the interconnected web they are a part of and realize they are an important part of a much bigger picture.

ROCKIES.AUDUBON.ORG

Grace
Ge Gabriel

Regional Director, International Fund For Animal Welfare, Asia

Grace Ge Gabriel is the driving force behind International Fund for Animal Welfare in China, where policies regarding conservation and animal welfare were lacking. She was instrumental in linking wildlife protection with development in the rural Yunnan province where the remaining Asian elephants roam. As a strong voice in the fight to reduce the devastating impact wildlife trade has on tigers, elephants, rhinos, bears and many other endangered species, she has testified before the European Union Commission and the UK Parliament Environmental Audit Committee.

How I Stay Inspired

THE MEASURABLE IMPACTS FROM our comprehensive approach to reducing wildlife trade in China, by influencing both market supply and consumer demand, keep me inspired. Utilizing public outreach, community mobilization, and policy advocacy (the three pillars of our behavior change campaign), International Fund for Animal Welfare (IFAW) was able to enhance policy, making marketplaces unavailable for wildlife trade, improve enforcement effectiveness, and motivate consumers to reject ivory consumption.

To reduce demand, we conduct public campaigns raising awareness about the link between ivory trade and elephant poaching. The campaign message resonated with the public so much that it got an ivory carver to put down his knife, an ivory consumer to reject ivory jewelry on social media and an ivory trader to expose the illegal ivory trade to the media. In four years, the "Mom, I have teeth" ad campaign reached 75 percent of urban China and reduced the group with the most propensity to purchase ivory from 54 percent to 26 percent.

I am constantly inspired by the behavior changes that happen at every level in society. Policy makers condemn and ban the trade of endangered species. Judiciary officials deliver harsh penalties to wildlife criminals. Corporations sponsor wildlife campaigns with enormous in-kind contribution. And a young boy's hunger strike forced his father to sign a family pledge rejecting ivory trade! Each of these actions, big or small, reaffirms my determination to stigmatize wildlife trade. To save wildlife species we have to make the consumption of their parts and products socially unacceptable.

IFAW.ORG/UNITED-STATES/ABOUT-US/
ELEPHANTS/GRACE-GE-GABRIEL

Kushal Sarma

Wildlife Veterinarian, India

Throughout India they call him the Elephant Doctor. Dr. Kushal Konwar Sarma is the veterinarian who gets the call when a rampaging bull elephant is wreaking havoc in a local community. With the world record for restraining and treating rogue tuskers, Dr. Sarma has saved countless elephants and humans and has paved a path for elephant conservation throughout Asia.

How I Stay Inspired

※

IN INDIA PEOPLE FIND it hard to believe that I joined the veterinary profession by choice, over medicine, engineering and pharmacy. The animals need for sincere care and doctoring I felt from my childhood. I live in a small village in the state of Assam, where people keep all sorts of different animals — cattle, buffaloes, goats, dogs, ducks, chickens, pigeons, and even elephants. I have seen their sufferings from injuries and diseases. I have seen them dying in epidemics, which probably motivated me to become an animal doctor. I remember how my siblings and I cried inconsolably at the sudden death of our dearest calf *Phool* (flower); we could not eat our meals for a couple of days.

It has been over three decades since I became a vet. My work schedule is 24/7. I teach veterinary surgery and radiology in the Guwahati Veterinary College for a living, but I like to be regarded as a doctor of animals. My pleasure lies in relieving an animal of its pain, whatever the species may be. But people associate my name more with the elephants. I get calls for elephants from all over Assam and other Indian states. It is indeed a great feeling to have my name associated with such a magnificent animal. However, time is my biggest constraint; often I drive overnight to attend a sick elephant hundreds of kilometers away from the city. My colleagues and students whom I leave the previous evening have no clue about my overnight mission when they see me in college the next morning.

What keeps me motivated? When I put that question to myself, I do not get a straight answer. My desire to relieve the sufferings of an animal? Or my desire for recognition in the society? Earn some extra money for my children? What keeps coming up for me are those instances where I gladly paid out of my own pocket to the mother of poor hungry children who did not have even a grain for dinner, after performing a caesarian operation on their only cow. Probably the age-old Indian value of deriving pleasure from giving, and not from taking, is flowing through my blood. My practice gives me the opportunity to give; could that be my only motivation? May be. And what about that glance of gratitude that I saw in the eyes of the electrocuted wild bull elephant in the Paneri tea estate that I could save from the quagmire of certain death? And what about the sweet embrace of the elephant Lakhimai in the circus performing at Himmatnagar in Gujarat, 2000km away from her sweet birthplace? Needless to mention that I was her regular vet and once cured her from a nagging wound on her back before she was sold to the circus. I feel the answer to how I stay inspired lies in the animals' repayment for my service in a much richer way, with their expression of love and gratitude.

ELEPHANTDOCTOR.ORG

Priscilla Feral

President, Friends Of Animals, USA

Priscilla Feral has presided over U.S. based Friends of Animals, an international non-profit animal advocacy organization, since 1987. She has also served as president of the San Antonio Sanctuary since 2007, which operates as a subsidiary of Friends of Animals. Friends of Animals places critical habitat, wildlife protection, veganism, environmental and animal rights issues at the core of animal advocacy. As a food activist, she has authored three vegan cookbooks for Friends of Animals, *Dining with Friends: The Art of North American Vegan Cuisine (2010)*, *The Best of Vegan Cooking (2009)*, and *For the Love of Dog Biscuits (2015)*.

How I Stay Inspired

SOCIAL MOVEMENTS, WHERE PEOPLE work for changes with other committed people to bring about positive changes in a society, are powerful. I find that inspiring, to give an intelligent effort my best shot.

Giving up isn't an option. My animal rights work isn't about me; I'm not a victim. Inspiration comes from not watering down principles, yet realizing that fundamental change is hard for people; many lack the discipline to disrupt their comfort zone. That kind of change comes from inspiration; how to identify success on one's own terms. I believe we need to operate on an assumption of success rather than failure. We have to listen as much as we're talking, to work on our personalities to be assertive, resilient, and inclusive, to win the public on one's view of a problem and solution. Moreover, it's helpful to have a sense of humor, to have some fun while trying, as the Texas writer Molly Ivins said, "to stave off the forces of darkness." The key to inspiration in this business is to take risks, not rest on my laurels, stay curious, and engage.

FRIENDSOFANIMALS.ORG

FACT FINDERS

There is a science behind saving wildlife and wild places. The conservationists in this section are conserving biodiversity worldwide through a combination of fieldwork, research, and education. It is not only their work that makes an impact. Studies show that simply the presence of conservation research projects in an area creates a positive impact on the wildlife and habitat: It acts as a deterrent to poachers, aids community awareness and involvement in conservation, and increases the value of species to local people.

Meg Lowman

Chief of Science & Sustainability, California Academy Of Sciences, USA

Nicknamed "Einstein of the treetops" by the Wall Street Journal, Margaret Lowman pioneered the science of tree canopy ecology. For over 30 years, she has designed hot-air balloons and walkways for treetop exploration to solve mysteries in the world's forests, especially insect pests and ecosystem health. In Dr. Lowman's current role as chief of science and sustainability at the California Academy of Sciences, she is responsible for the Academy's programs of scientific research and exploration, as well as its programs addressing the challenge of sustaining life on earth.

How I Stay Inspired

I ADMIT THAT TROPICAL forest conservation is a fairly depressing profession right now, with the plight of deforestation, and that there is no payoff in terms of dollars and cents in the world of science; but I get my inspiration from two things: 1) As a mom, it means a lot to me if I can leave the planet a better place for my children; and 2) as a scientist, who devotes much of her time in emerging cultures, such as India and Ethiopia, I feel a true sense of passion to serve as a role model and inspiration for all the women in those countries, who represent 51 percent of our global IQ and yet have relatively few opportunities, unless we empower them.

In my work at the California Academy of Sciences, I am optimistic that we can reach a bigger and more diverse public with the museum platform, including education about the importance of forests and the values they provide to human health. With both virtual reach and museum exhibits and publications, we can take on big challenges such as tropical rain forest conservation.

Personally, I live by the mantra that was expressed in the last two sentences of my book, *Life in the Treetops:* "One of the most meaningful insights that I have acquired along my life's journey is that it takes the same amount of energy to complain as it does to exclaim—but the results are incredibly different. Learning to exclaim instead of complain has been my most valuable lesson."

CANOPYMEG.COM
CALACADEMY.ORG/LOWMAN

Frank Lance Craighead

Executive Director, Craighead Institute, USA

Frank Lance Craighead grew up helping his father, Frank, and uncle, John, with their pioneering study of grizzly bears in Yellowstone Park in the early 1960's. As a field ecologist, population geneticist and GIS technician, he is a research affiliate in the ecology department at Montana State University and a member of the IUCN World Committee on Protected Areas, the Society for Conservation Biology, and the Society for Conservation GIS. The Craighead Institute develops and implements conservation plans across multiple scales. Grizzly bears have always been a central focus. He co-edited *Conservation Planning: Shaping the Future*, (2013).

How I Stay Inspired

WILDLIFE AND WILD PLACES are being squeezed out of
existence by a human population and its ubiquitous footprint
on the planet. The extinction rate is at an all-time high and
continues to accelerate. Global warming is here and will only
get much worse, even if we could somehow stop adding CO_2
to the atmosphere tomorrow. War and civil unrest is spreading
and wildlife casualties are collateral damage that is ignored
in the light of the human suffering that occurs. Even in the
United States, wildlife faces escalating competition for the use
of secure habitat and wild places; aggressive backcountry rec-
reation demands are gradually reducing the carrying capacity of even protected places; development demands, even for
clean energy facilities, are fragmenting whatever habitat is left.
Where is there a shred of hope?

Given these current conditions it is hard to be inspired
to work for a healthy planet and abundant wildlife, but what
else are you going to do? If you're not part of the solution you
are part of the problem. Nobody who can think clearly about

the state of the planet wants to be part of the problem. The overriding issue is that there don't seem to be a lot of people who are thinking clearly about the state of the planet. This is an issue that can be addressed; we need to hope that if people can learn how serious the situation is, they will change their behavior to reduce their demands on this finite planet. This is where I find my inspiration. I put my hope in my 13-year old daughter and her friends; and their friends; and their cohorts around the world. They are learning rapidly.

The people who are causing environmental damage are we, the "grown-ups." Some of us can change, but most of us won't. Some of us are causing incredible damage through the corporations and governments, industries and institutions that they control; but they won't live forever. They may not even be in control as long as they live. It is my hope that the young people around the world will realize what is wrong, who is to blame, and what they have to do in order to survive. First of all, they need to keep the life-support systems of the planet, the natural ecosystems that still function, healthy and protected. And they need to live with lighter footprints on the planet. If they already are barely surviving, they need to learn to coexist within the ecosystems they inhabit, and not destroy them. I believe that young people can do that. We just need to help them realize that it is necessary; there is no other reasonable option.

I am inspired by small victories and little discoveries. I am inspired to learn that Chernobyl has been populated with wildlife, by blooms in the desert, by grizzly bears showing up in new places, and by sea turtles rescued from nets. I cheer the rejection of the Keystone pipeline, the Papal Encyclical on Climate Change, and Doctors/Engineers/Teachers without borders. The degradation of our planetary environment is so widespread and intense that it cannot be reversed overnight, or even in my lifetime. Things can only be improved slowly and incrementally over a long period of time; but further damage has to be limited immediately. I'm hoping that the kids will take over right away.

CRAIGHEADINSTITUTE.ORG

Joyce Poole

Co-Founder, Elephant Voices, Kenya

One of the world's foremost authorities on elephants, Dr. Joyce Poole holds a PhD in elephant behavior from Cambridge University and has studied the social behavior and communication of African elephants for over forty years. Dr. Poole's work and discoveries about the minds and behavior of this fascinating and threatened species has been documented in numerous popular articles and film documentaries, scores of scientific publications and two books she authored, *Coming of Age with Elephants* and *Elephants*. In 2011 she and her husband, Petter Granli, founded Elephant Voices (in Kenya) to further their scientific and conservation work.

How I Stay Inspired

I HAVE A STRONG inner drive and an exuberant personality, characteristics that run in my family. I am passionate about elephants, indeed all animals, and the wild places where they are found–perhaps because these elements were such a meaningful part of my upbringing. The world is changing so fast now as human populations expand and demand for resources grows. The things I love are being squeezed out at an alarming rate, and the consequences for individual animals, their families, and the habitats they depend on, is devastating.

I am inspired to try to bring about respect for nature by sharing my passion and my experiences with others.

ELEPHANTVOICES.ORG

Amanda Stronza

Environmental Anthropologist & Professor,
Texas A&M University, USA

Dr. Amanda Stronza is an environmental anthropologist and associate professor at Texas A&M University, where she co-founded and co-directs the National Science Foundation-IGERT Program in Applied Biodiversity Science. For over 20 years, she has led research on community-based conservation, ecotourism and sustainable development, mostly in the Amazon. Amanda is currently a co-director for the Ecoexist Project in Botswana, working to find ways to reduce human-elephant conflicts in the Okavango Delta.

How I Stay Inspired

AS AN ANTHROPOLOGIST, MY inspiration comes from seeing wildlife and wild places through the eyes of people who know them best. After years in the classroom, my most important understandings of the world have come from living outside and learning among rural and indigenous peoples: the Ese eja, Ribereños, Achuar, and Tacana of the Amazon, the Hambukushu, Bayei, and Basarwa of the Okavango, the Agta of the Philippines, and the Dayak of Indonesia, among others. They represent different traditions and different environments, but they all experience nature and culture as entwined. They know directly the sources of their water, food, and shelter. They live where animals, wild and domestic, breathe, bleat, and roar within earshot of each other.

Most of our work in conservation is focused necessarily on communities — communities of people, communities of animals, and the aggregates of all of them across time and space. As scientists, we focus wide, over eons and biomes, seeking trends and patterns. And we require sample sizes big enough to give us rigor and reliability in our forecasts and models.

But I find hope in the small and the singular. In homes around the world and in the U.S., I've learned to see conservation by paying attention to the one—the one moment, the one place, the one person.

We have license to do that in anthropology. Life histories and memories, traditions, norms, beliefs, and even music, dance and art, are all data that illuminate the world for us. They tell us about human-environment relationships and how, when and why, people care about forests, wildlife, rivers, and shores. They help us see and understand the farmer who nurtures as much as cultivates his land, the hunter who embodies and moves with the forest rather than merely through it, the mother who remains connected with the wild gardens behind her home, returning again and again for medicine, seeds, roots, fibers, and sacred space. For every story of degradation, greed, or disregard, these stories of stewardship and connection help us stay inspired.

When I listen to the experiences of rural and traditional peoples around the world who live closest to the animals and places that mean the most to me, I often find myself in tears— not from despair, but from a heart full of hope.

BIODIVERSITY.TAMU.EDU
ECOEXISTPROJECT.ORG

Anthony Collins

Director Of Baboon Research, Gombe Stream
Research Centre, Tanzania

Since 1972, Anthony Collins has conducted the long-term study of baboons with a team of Tanzanian field assistants at Gombe Stream National Park, and assisted in management of the Gombe Stream Research Centre—its staff and visiting researchers, in their studies of chimpanzees, guenon monkeys, vegetation, primate diets, and primate health. Linking the research with the youth branch (Roots & Shoots) and the Community Conservation branch (TACARE) of the Jane Goodall Institute, Tanzania, and representing the Institute, and Jane Goodall herself, to local community and government and to all collaborators, donors and other visitors.

How I Stay Inspired

PROTECTION MUST BE GIVEN to all forms of life, as they have a right to continue to exist here on earth. They and their lineages have been here millions of years and many of them have been here many times longer than we have. Our children need them too, and deserve to have them to share the planet.

It's also true that the people among whom we work, in a very rural and poor area of Africa, need them too, although many of them do not know it or do not think so. In fact, the survival of ecosystems and natural biodiversity in every landscape is essential for society as a whole.

What I believe, and what we can hope people who destroy living things and pillage ecosystems can also come to believe, is that we depend on our natural surroundings. We are part of the world's ecology and we cannot replace it; we must live sustainably within it. What we see clearly where I work in western Tanzania is that diverse and functioning woodlands, forests and grasslands are essential to the cycling of water, the rainfall which farmers depend on, the stream flow which villagers depend on, the stability of the soil against erosion . . . these things can be obvious to all and are quite easy to teach.

Less visible things–the production of oxygen by plants, the buffering against global climate change by the sheer volume of the natural vegetation in woodlands and forests, their function as a haven for pollinators and seed-dispersers and insect-eaters which allow people to harvest from the land, the protective-ness of species-richness against pathogens, the capacity of the land to absorb and negate the waves of pollutants and refuse we leave — these things need to be explained and demonstrated over time.

My day-to-day commitment is renewed by the sheer beauty of natural things, their changes from morning to night, their differences each day, from season to season; the feel of the air and its fragrances; the beauty of plants as they grow, burst into leaf, flower, fruit, and fall; and the insects and birds they harbor. These things, which surround us continually or which surprise us unawares, serve to raise the spirits, and to remind and justify all the reasons I have given above.

JANEGOODALL.ORG

Lisa Dabek

Senior Conservation Scientist, Woodland Park Zoo, USA

Lisa Dabek is senior conservation scientist at the Woodland Park Zoo (WPZ) in Seattle, Washington and founded and is director of their community-based Tree Kangaroo Conservation Program (TKCP) in Papua New Guinea (PNG). In 2013 an independent NGO was formed in PNG called TKCP-PNG for which she is the chair of the board of directors. She and the team work in partnership with indigenous landowners, scientists, students, educators, government officials and healthcare professionals from the U.S., Australia and PNG to study and protect the wildlife and rainforest habitat of PNG and support the local communities. In 2009 TKCP and the local community created PNG's first conservation area, protecting over 180,000 acres of rainforest.

How I Stay Inspired

TREE KANGAROOS ARE FASCINATING animals, and that is what brought me to Papua New Guinea (PNG) to study and conserve them. I always say that the tree kangaroos brought me to PNG, yet it's the local indigenous people that I work with that keep me there and are so inspiring to me. The opportunity to work collaboratively with the local communities to make sure the tree kangaroos are protected and do not go extinct, while making sure there is support for these remote communities, is incredibly gratifying. I was raised to give back to the world in some way; this is a way that I can contribute to the world and help wildlife and people. As difficult and trying as the work is sometimes, there isn't a day that goes by that I do not feel lucky to be able to do the work I do. We have made great strides in conservation and now our program and team is a model for the country. That is very inspiring!

After 20 years of working in PNG as founder and Director of the Tree Kangaroo Conservation Program in Yopno-Uruwa-Som (YUS), I am just as enthusiastic about the work as when I started. Getting to keep going into the forest and do fieldwork definitely keeps me going and energized. Now I also focus more on mentoring the next generation of conservation leaders in PNG, which is very inspiring in a different way. Conservation is about people and I am continually moved and inspired by the people of YUS and PNG.

ZOO.ORG/TREE

Colleen Begg

Co-Founder, Niassa Lion Project, Mozambique

South African conservation biologists Keith and Colleen Begg met next to an elephant carcass in South Africa's Kruger National Park more than twenty years ago and have been studying and protecting carnivores together ever since. Their first great love was the honey badger. At present, their focus is African lions. However, they are concerned about all carnivores and have worked on cheetah, mink, marten and, for many years, the honey badger. Since 2003 they have been working in Niassa National Reserve in northern Mozambique as the Niassa Carnivore Project.

How I Stay Inspired

THE IUCN RED DATA list estimates that there are only 20–30,000 lions left in Africa. I have learned to not think of the big picture because it can be too overwhelming. Instead, I focus on small successes. It's the small successes that excite and inspire me. For instance, there was one young man from the community who wanted to take the training from us to be a scout, but we didn't think he would be good at it. He kept insisting, and we put him in the 45-day intensive course. While he was there his father died, yet he was so committed to the course that he did not go back home for the funeral. He told us his father would be proud of him. He passed the course, and he, and others like him, are an inspiration to me. With enough time and experience I believe we can make conservationists out of people. People can learn to care.

I have met some poachers and have empathy for them. Poaching is survival, and people are not against the animal. I believe that if we can increase food security and provide alternative livelihoods through conservation agriculture, small livestock breeding and our elephant bee hive fences (based on the work of Save the Elephants and Lucy King) for stopping the biggest crop raiders, the elephants, we have hope for the future.

What's the alternative anyway; to give up? That is not an option. I have to continue to find small success stories and use those to inspire me to continue to move forward with our work.

NIASSALION.ORG

FOUNDERS

*The conservationists in this group have started
their own NGOs and in most cases are actively involved
in running those organizations. They are creative, wildly
driven for their causes, and possess entrepreneurial spirits.
These are the masterminds behind some of the most
effective NGOs worldwide.*

Kristine McDivitt Tompkins

Founder, Conservacion Patagonia, Patagonia

Kristine McDivitt Tompkins is a conservationist and former CEO of Patagonia, Inc. Since 1993, she has worked with her husband, Douglas Tompkins, to create new national parks in Chile and Argentina. Together they have protected over 2.2 million acres, more land than any other private individuals. The Tompkins have donated three national parks (two in Chile and one in Argentina) with an additional seven more in the works. In 2000 Kris founded Conservacion Patagonica to create national parks in Patagonia that save and restore wild lands and wildlife, inspire care for the natural world, and generate healthy economic opportunities for local communities. For their conservation work, Kris and Doug have received Scenic Hudson's Visionary Conservationist Award, the African Rainforest Conservancy's New Species Award, and Latin Trade's "Environmental Leader of the Year" award, among others.

How I Stay Inspired

OFTENTIMES I THINK I'M motivated less by inspiration than I am by my sense of urgency that those things I love in the non-human world are disappearing very, very rapidly, so every day counts. Of course, I have been inspired by many individuals who have been on the front lines of land and species conservation for the last hundred years, and I marvel at the foresight they had to detect the probability of destruction of the natural world long ago before the signs of our modern-day disregard for the importance of healthy biotic communities was in such stark evidence. Of course, a big part of our work is found in the creation of new national parks, so we look to 2016, the 100th anniversary of the US National Park system (when Theodore Roosevelt inaugurated Yellowstone National Park) as a beacon for our work.

I am inspired by those who have had the means to do great conservation on a grand scale, but equally inspired by individuals who, with more determination than financial means, have dedicated their lives to protecting the non-human world that has no voice.

The second inspiration is my network. I have surrounded myself, both professionally and personally, with a network of supporters. Notice that I said personally, as well. You don't have to work within the conservation field in order to have an impact. In fact, I believe you can have a bigger impact at times when you are "outside" the conservation world, looking in. But in a world where nature dances with politics and is mixed by science, you have to have a network. Whether it is friends, family, or faith, my support network helps me through those rough days.

Finally, my faith. Raised Catholic, now Unitarian Universalist, I rely on my faith to "pull me through," so to speak. My belief that I am a small, but important, part of something bigger and that my actions will be supported, gave me the foundation from which my roots have grown strong. Faith has strengthened my fortitude, so when adversity hits, I am able to sit for a quiet moment and know that I am supported and that although I may get knocked around, I will not be knocked over. My faith gives me the support I need to make hard decisions, and of course to keep moving forward through good times and bad. I know it seems a little out of place for a conservationist, a scientist, to speak of faith, but for me the mere fact that I am not in this alone makes every day easier.

TOMPKINSCONSERVATION.ORG

Alasdair
Harris

Executive Director, Blue Ventures, UK

A marine ecologist with an unhealthy obsession for corals, Alasdair Harris founded U.K. based Blue Ventures to demonstrate that effective marine conservation requires pragmatic, entrepreneurial and community-based approaches to coastal management. He is a visiting post-doctoral researcher at the University of Oxford's Environmental Change Institute, a member of the World Commission on Protected Areas, and a technical advisor to the United Nations Environment Program's Convention on Migratory Species Secretariat.

How I Stay Inspired

I DERIVE MUCH OF my inspiration from observing nature's incredible ability to regenerate and bounce back. Whether it's the way life and abundance return in spring, or the way wilderness recovers in a protected area—the unstoppable resilience of nature on the rebound is a source of great hope.

I was lucky enough to do my PhD in the British Indian Ocean Territory, the world's largest coral atoll. It's a place of incredible marine diversity, extremely remote and almost entirely uninhabited, but was devastated in 1998 by a severe ocean-warming episode linked to the El Nino event, causing widespread mortality of corals. Less than ten years later I was able to document the recovery of this system back to a thriving reef community with prolific coral growth—an incredible example of nature's resilience.

BLUEVENTURES.ORG

Claudine Andre

Founder and Director, Lola ya Bonobo, Congo

In 2002, Claudine Andre opened Lola ya Bonobo, the only bonobo sanctuary in the world, just outside of Kinshasa. But her reach extends beyond her sanctuary, to the rest of the Congo. Working with a formidable team, she is devoted to educating the Congolese about the preciousness of the endangered bonobo and the danger and cruelty of eating bush meat.

How I Stay Inspired

❧

I KNEW NOTHING ABOUT bonobos fifteen years ago. It all started when I was given an orphan bonobo called Mikeno when I was volunteering at the Kinshasa zoo during 1993, while we had a difficult political period where there was looting. I collected food from the only two local restaurants to feed starving animals at the zoo. During this time, a friend brought me Mikeno. Further north, starving soldiers were shooting bonobos for food, and before long, more bonobo orphans found their way to me.

I wanted a paradise for them, somewhere they could always see the sky. And so I created Lola ya Bonobo. This is what keeps me going in the end. This animal is so fragile, but so fascinating. I keep hope alive by always trying to do more, to do better.

We run many different conservation programs besides those for the orphans at the sanctuary. We have over 30,000 Congolese visitors a year, most of them school children who have never seen a bonobo before. We also send education officers to classrooms in Kinshasa to teach children about bonobos, because children are Congo's future, and it will be them who decide whether or not to eat bonobos in the future. We also send education officers into the heart of the country, along the bush meat trade routes. They talk to hunters and civil servants, start education programs in the villages, and convince local chiefs to persuade their community members that the bonobos are a treasure that are uniquely Congolese, that they should be proud of.

Everywhere we go, we organize meetings with civil servants, military — everyone who is a decider. When we began, bonobos were not well known. Now they are better known throughout Congo.

We also have successfully become the first to release bonobos back into the wild. One day, if Lola's bonobos are all we have left, we will hopefully have developed a method to successfully release them into the wild and refill Congo's empty forests.

LOLAYABONOBO.ORG

Ric
O'Barry

Founder, The Ric O'Barry Dolphin Project, USA

Ric O'Barry has worked on both sides of the captive dolphin issue, including training the five dolphins who played the role of *Flipper* in the popular U.S. television series of the same name. On the first Earth Day, in 1970, he launched the Dolphin Project against the multi-billion-dollar dolphin captivity industry, and has been going at it ever since. He was named *Huffington Post's*" 2010 Most Influential Green Game Changer," and listed on *O Magazine's* "2010 Power List — Men We Admire." He is the star of the Academy Award-winning documentary *The Cove* and the Animal Planet television series *Blood Dolphin$*, and the author of *Behind the Dolphin Smile* and *To Free A Dolphin*.

How I Stay Inspired

〰

WHEN I STARTED THE Dolphin Project a couple of decades ago, I was coming from a place of guilt and anger. *Flipper,* the television series I was the dolphin trainer for, created this multi-million dollar industry of capturing dolphins. I felt guilty when I saw things like Brazil's last captive dolphin, living in a cesspool, named Flipper. I know why they named it Flipper, and it was my guilt that inspired me to keep going.

These days I'm inspired by the changes I see. We have made progress. I would have dropped out long ago if I didn't see results. I see change all the time.

I have witnessed many people change after watching the documentaries *The Cove* and *Blackfish.* Bearing witness to something makes a powerful impact on people. *The Cove* has created many activists, and *Black Fish* has educated many people about the realities of marine parks. Sea World attendance is down as a result. Those are the kinds of changes that inspire me to keep going.

DOLPHINPROJECT.NET

〰

Laurie Marker

Founder and Executive Director,
Cheetah Conservation Fund, Namibia

Having worked with cheetahs since 1974, Laurie Marker set up the Cheetah Conservation Fund in 1990 and moved to Namibia to develop a permanent conservation research center for the wild cheetah. Dr. Marker was recognized as one of *Time Magazine's* Heroes for the Planet in 2000 and received the Zoological Society of San Diego's Lifetime Achievement Award in 2008. More recently, she was awarded the 2010 Tyler Prize for Environmental Achievement and was a finalist for the BBC World Challenge.

How I Stay Inspired

I FIRST CAME TO Namibia in 1977, and this is when I learned that livestock farmers considered cheetahs vermin. They were killing cheetahs by the hundreds each year. Then, when I moved to Namibia for good in 1991 — an American woman trying to save cheetahs — most farmers wondered why I was so interested in both the cheetahs and, equally, local farmers. They thought I was strange, but I sat with them, listened to them, and learned everything I could from them about good or inefficient farming practices. You couldn't find more negative attitudes in some of them, but I listened because I knew in their minds they had valid reasons to shoot cheetahs. I didn't want to judge. I wanted to try and understand so we could work together toward a balanced future. I guess it was all about determination. I don't allow any negativity to stop the course of my work. I can't allow anything to affect my inspiration, because the cheetah doesn't have time.

CHEETAH.ORG

David
Shepherd

Founder, David Shepherd Wildlife Foundation,
South Africa

David Shepherd was an artist until a fateful day in 1960, when the sight of 255 zebra dead around a waterhole, poisoned by poachers, turned him into a conservationist. Since then he has used his art to raise funds for wildlife, and in 1984 he started his own South African foundation to continue and consolidate his passion to protect endangered wildlife. In June 2008 he received a CBE for services to conservation. At 84, David continues to paint for family and friends and helps to raise funds for his foundation, which supports projects across Africa and Asia.

How I Stay Inspired

❦

IT WAS MORE THAN 30 years ago that I wept in the back of my safari vehicle at the sight of an elephant hobbling along on three feet, a landmine having blown its foot off. It was moments like that, and many others, including seeing 255 dead zebra at a poisoned waterhole, that inspired me to become a conservationist. Working to protect wildlife is never an easy job. There are as many lows as highs. The lows are deep; there can be nothing worse than the news that a species has become extinct or that nothing seems to have been done to protect a vulnerable species. The highs, while euphoric, can be fleeting; for all the great news that a vulnerable population is increasing, there is the difficult job of securing the funding to continue the vital protection measures to ensure that the population remains safe.

In my lifetime I have experienced a thousand highs and lows when it comes to wildlife conservation and people often ask me how have I maintained my enthusiasm, how have I stayed inspired. There is one fundamental ingredient that keeps me inspired — passion. I have the deepest passion for wildlife, all wildlife, and I have passion for this beautiful planet. I am also passionate about the terrible mess that mankind seems to be making of it! I once had the honor of meeting the American astronaut Neil Armstrong, who described to me how fragile the planet looked when he was coming back to earth from space. We have this arrogant assumption that man can treat the world just as he wishes. What we need to understand is that we don't own the planet. We share it.

While some issues seem insurmountable, I remain optimistic on many levels. One of the things that keeps me optimistic is the younger generation. Imagine the feelings of sheer joy when through our Global Canvas competition we received six drawings from Russian children in Vladivostok asking, "Please help us to save our tigers." It made me so emotional it moved me to tears. It is moments like that that keep me inspired.

My foundation now runs an annual art and poetry competition for under 16-year-olds called Global Canvas, and the quality of the entries we receive from around the world is amazing. In every brush stroke and poem you can sense a deep understanding of the issues facing our planet and it is my greatest hope that those young people will continue to carry the torch for wildlife and inspire many generations to come to do the same. A world without wildlife is simply too bleak to contemplate.

DAVIDSHEPHERD.ORG

Bonnie Vyper

Founder, Thinking Animals, USA

Bonnie Wyper is co-founder and president of Thinking Animals United (TAU), a New York City-based non-profit organization that produces the lecture series "Exploring Animal Minds." TAU is also producing the ReThinking Animals Summit in 2016, the most diverse and comprehensive gathering to date of global experts in research, conservation and the humane treatment of animals, in conversation with leaders in business, government, media, education, theology, and the arts to challenge our current understanding of animals and their environments.

How I Stay Inspired

I LOVE WHAT I do, and sincerely believe I can make a difference in the lives of animals. I am horrified by what we as humans do to other species, not only to wildlife and their environments, but also to captive animals on factory farms, in labs, circuses and aquaria. Each animal is an individual with its own will to experience the life it was born to have. I get scores of emails everyday showing how we prevent this from happening in the most brutal, inhumane, and sickening ways possible. I have learned not to look at these images. In the past, I have—and I still have nightmares about what I saw. It brings out the most violent aspect of being human in me: I want to kill the person who has harmed these animals. The images haunt me for years.

What keeps me going is the belief that I can actually make a difference. I feel in some ways I don't have any choice but to do this, because I have an obligation to do so (lucky I love it!). I know that it takes generations to change attitudes, but in the four years since I started Thinking Animals in order to share scientific research on the intelligence and emotional lives of animals, I have seen an explosion of interest in animals. There is more press, more animal studies programs, and more of an emphasis on humane education, and more people volunteering to help animals. Worldwide there are efforts being undertaken to measure the full economic impact of development on conservation and biodiversity. People are more willing to confront the moral and ethical impact of our relations with other species, how our lives are intertwined, and what effects of doing nothing to prevent their slaughter will have on our own lives. The next generation is so much more informed about the issues than we were at their age. They use new technologies that we didn't have. This gives me a real sense that we can change the current crises for animals. We just need to hammer away, each doing what we can to add our efforts to the fight, and it gives me huge pleasure to do so.

So I ask myself: "What does it take to change people's attitudes so that they will accept their individual responsibility to other species; to recognize that we each have a moral and ethical choice to help or not help those who cannot challenge our destruction of their lives and homes?" Knowing the answer to that question—that it takes each one of us to take just one step to help—and believing that an increasing number of people are doing so, keeps me going.

THINKINGANIMALS.ORG

Natalie Kyriacou

Founder and Director, My Green World, Australia

As the founder of My Green World, Natalie Kyriacou believes in empowering people from all over the world to take part in wildlife and environmental conservation initiatives. Kyriacou is the creator of the mobile game app World of the Wild and is on the board of directors of Dogstar Foundation. She has worked as a freelance journalist for a range of publications; her passion led her to write about wildlife and environmental issues. Natalie was selected as Australia's "Social Pioneer" in 2015 and is committed to developing innovative and educational platforms to enhance the efforts of global wildlife and environmental conservation.

How I Stay Inspired

HALF OF THE WORLD'S species have disappeared in the last forty years. Approximately 95 elephants are killed every day. And terrible atrocities being committed against our natural world continue to make headlines every day. Despite this, I remain optimistic and utterly inspired by the many wonderful people who dedicate their time to creating a better future for all of earth's inhabitants. I am constantly encouraged by the hearty dialogue, the creative exchange of ideas, and the compassion that the international community has shown toward other beings.

For every one person that is acting illegally or unethically towards wildlife, there are thousands of people who are fighting against it. For every one person that isn't aware of the plight of our world's wildlife, there are thousands of people trying to educate them. It is the individual acts of bravery that inspire me, along with the knowledge that such bravery is bringing our society together in a collaborative, compassionate space to make a difference.

And of course, the most inspiring thing of all is to witness a wild animal live free in its natural, flourishing environment, and know that I, along with many others, am trying my very hardest to secure that animal's future.

MYGREENWORLD.ORG

Mary Hutton

Founder and Chairperson, Free The Bears, Australia

Mary Hutton was born in the United Kingdom and immigrated with her family to Perth, Western Australia in 1970. When she is not travelling to South-East Asia to visit Free The Bears sanctuaries she is working in the office, planning the next fundraiser for the organization, which is dedicated to protecting, preserving, and enriching the lives of bears throughout the world. Nominated by the Australia Day Council in 2015 for Australian of the Year, Hutton was also awarded both the Environment Medal and the People's Choice Award in the 2015 Pride of Australia medals ceremony, and most recently she won the Jeanne Marchig Animal Welfare Award.

How I Stay Inspired

PASSION, COMMITMENT AND A very strong determination go hand in hand with the word "inspired." One cannot be inspired without other emotions.

I stay inspired to continue to save the bears because I have seen what a difference one can make. Once they have been rescued these poor bears continue to inspire me with their courage to live after years of abuse and maltreatment and their wonderful ability to forgive.

There will always be negative issues facing wildlife and the bears. The problems seem insurmountable, but how can one give up, knowing there are animals suffering every day at the hands of the poachers? It is with this in mind that I continue to work for bears, aware that they have inspired me to actually do something, and that this inspiration has shown me the right way to approach governments in order to work with them to help the bears.

FREETHEBEARS.ORG

Eli
Weiss

Founder and President WildiZe Foundation, USA

Combining her love of Africa, wildlife, art, environmental ethics and conservation, Eli Weiss founded the U.S. based non-profit WildiZe Foundation in 2000, providing targeted grant funding to individuals and educational institutions dedicated to the conservation of wildlife, wildlife habitats and the indigenous cultures of Africa through building on-the-ground relationships and projects. Weiss is the host of the Our Wild World radio show, interviewing leaders in the conservation field about creative solutions based on science, the environment and culture, to make conservation a lifestyle.

How I Stay Inspired

WHAT KEEPS ME INSPIRED? Our human spirit and our resilience. What keeps me motivated? My anger, and channeling it into supporting creative new models and solutions by those who see what is being lost. When I was young and starting out, I never imagined that all our combined genius as a species would turn us into a viral and single minded mass in quest of total consumption, to the point that we would destroy the very fabrics of societies and our planet, that with all the knowledge we had back then, and all the knowledge we have now, we would simply be so stupid and short term in our thinking. My viewpoint today has almost shifted right back to the beginning: the recognition that conservation is a necessary lifestyle. I do believe we will come to our senses–hopefully within my lifetime and without much further species loss.

Inspiration comes in the small moments and knowing there is a shift in consciousness. Earth is hiring. Young minds are blending with unprecedented technology, an inspired mindfulness in conservation models, and lifestyles that reconnect us with the stunning magnificence, magnitude and beauty that is Life On Earth. Albeit kicking and screaming, we are forced by science, faith and young generations into grasping the concept that all life is inextricably linked and that, as always, humanity's needs and the needs of wildlife are one and the same: a healthy planet. I see this shift happening all around the world, and despite the horror of who we often are, I know that there are everyday heroes. And as long as we keep getting up and remembering that we have all the time in the world, as long as we start . . . . Now.

WILDIZE.ORG

VOICEAMERICA.COM/SHOW/2129/OUR-WILD-WORLD

SHOW AND TELL

---

*The authors, photographers, and videographers
in this section write the stories, take the photographs
and make the films that educate and enlighten
the world about conservation issues.*

Carl Safina

Founder and Director, Safina Center, USA

Carl Safina's writing has won the Lannan Literary Award and the John Burroughs, James Beard, and George Rabb medals. He has a PhD in ecology from Rutgers University. Safina is the inaugural endowed professor for nature and humanity at Stony Brook University and is founding president of the U.S. based not-for-profit Safina Center. He hosted the 10-part PBS series *Saving the Ocean with Carl Safina*. His seventh book is *Beyond Words; What Animals Think and Feel* (2015).

How I Stay Inspired

IT'S NOT SO MUCH that I "stay inspired;" it's that animals and the beauty of the real world continually inspire me. The seasons. The migrations, both subtle and spectacular. All the things that enliven the world. All are miraculous. The way the world renews itself. All of it energizes me.

I am not just talking about the grand things, like breaching whales and trumpeting elephants, though those surely qualify, and I've been lucky enough to spend real quality time in their presence. A chickadee at the feeder qualifies also. Most mornings in our suburban university neighborhood I just like to sit out back with my coffee, in the company of our doggies, watching our chickens pecking up breakfast in the yard and keeping an eye on the birds and squirrels. They are my meditation as well as my inspiration. Then I go to work and face whatever news comes my way as I try to craft some message or passage of response, using the words at my fingertips.

Yes, conservation is sometimes difficult and dispiriting. But I can't justify giving in to those feelings. For one thing,

I want to continue trying to help make things better. For another, how can I possibly justify feeling down? I am not one of the elephants in danger. I am not one of the desperate poachers or courageous rangers. I am safe. My life is fine. If reading and writing and working on conservation is too depressing, I have the option of pouring a glass of wine or getting some ice cream. There are many, many creatures and humans in real pain. I am not one of them, so I don't indulge my feelings when things seem — as they often do — overwhelming. I don't deserve the luxury of feeling like it's "too hard," because even when it feels that way, the fact is that, for me, it isn't. I have the perspective to realize this. And I have the privilege to work on things that really matter to me, the opportunity to help give voice to the voiceless. And I have the ability to take a walk around the pond, or along the beach, and watch for migrating loons. And then, back to work, newly inspired.

CARLSAFINA.ORG

BEYOND-WORDS.NET

Tom
Mangelsen

Images Of Nature Gallery, USA

Legendary American nature photographer Thomas D. Mangelsen has traveled for over 40 years observing and photographing the earth's last great wild places. From Artic polar bears to vast herds of African game, from South American jungles to the tigers of India, as well as the mosaic of animals inhabiting the American West, Mangelsen has captured rare moments and vast panoramas from all seven continents. His honors include Conservation Photographer of the Year (*Nature's Best Photography*), Wildlife Photographer of the Year (BBC), Outstanding Nature Photographer of the Year (NANPA), one of 100 Most Important People in Photography (*American Photo*), and one of 40 Most Influential Nature Photographers (*Outdoor Photography*). Major museums, including the Smithsonian's National Museum of Natural History, have exhibited his work which is collected by thousands worldwide from his galleries and website.

How I Stay Inspired

INSPIRATION COMES FROM MANY places, in many forms. It comes from history, from relationships with people, from connections to animals in the natural world, and from hope for the future.

So very many people have gone before us who have inspired better stewardship of the earth, who have inspired "conservation." Some have passed now, but some, like the seemingly immortal Jane Goodall, continue to challenge and motivate me into never giving up. Jane is the person that inspires me the most. She has a drive that is infectious; Jane simply does not allow me to get discouraged ... "We CAN'T give up, Tom."

And it is with Jane's words in my heart that I go out into the wildness, where the earth itself inspires me. Without wildness, I am incomplete; I flounder in a world where I cannot connect to wilderness and those that live harmoniously on its landscapes. My business has been built upon my ability to capture the images of nature with which I am able to share nature's beauty; yet for me, getting another photograph of a bear in Grand Teton National Park is not what takes me there . . . it is the communion of being in the presence of the bear that feeds my soul.

I have spent so many precious moments with bears, moments that have become hours, hours that have become days and days that have become years; yet exposure alone does not cement the inspiration the bears give me. If single events can "charge us up" and change our perspective, then my relationship to the iconic, elusive, and magnificent cougar is proof that inspiration is a powerful catalyst for conservation.

On Valentine's Day in 1999, a mother mountain lion and her three kittens stole my heart. Her mercurial appearance just one mile outside Jackson heralded the epitome of inspiration manifesting as action. After observing her for every one of the forty-two days that this beautiful creature graced us with her presence, I was moved to start The Cougar Fund with writer Cara Blessley Lowe. The Cougar Fund continues today as a passionate and effective symbol of how, when we act on what inspires us, we carve out a spot where change can happen.

I continue to be inspired, just as I was on a recent trip to Torres del Pine National Park in Chile. Expert trackers knowing their way around one of the most beautiful places on earth allowed me the privilege of refreshing the heart-swelling experience of seeing the Americas' greatest cat in the wild. In Chile they are known as puma, but they are the same glorious creatures that captivated me fifteen years before in Wyoming. It is as if the animals themselves are urging me on to speak the language of the heart that values them alive in this chaotic world of exploitation and dispassion.

This brings me to my least comfortable form of inspiration, which is when everything seems to be going badly. That is when I believe that change is bubbling up to happen and that it is the pressure of the status quo that keeps it from bursting through. Times of great strife herald times of great reward. It is just as Jane says: "We CAN'T give up, Tom."

MANGELSEN.COM

THECOUGARFUND.ORG

Richard
Louv

Co-Founder, Children & Nature Network, USA

Richard Louv is a journalist and author of eight books, including *Last Child in the Woods: Saving Our Children From Nature-Deficit Disorder* and *The Nature Principle: Reconnecting with Life in a Virtual Age.* He is co-founder and chairman emeritus of U.S. based Children & Nature Network, an organization helping build the international movement to connect people and communities to the natural world.

How I Stay Inspired

⁂

IN AN ESSAY I posted, called "Seven Reasons for a New Nature Movement," I paraphrased Martin Luther King Jr., who taught us that any movement — any culture — will fail if it cannot paint a picture of a world that people will want to go to. I wrote that, for many Americans, perhaps most, thinking about the future conjures up images of "Blade Runner" or "Mad Max," a post-apocalyptic dystopia stripped of nature, in which humans are stripped of their humanity. This is a dangerous fixation. One reason for it is the absence of what King advised: that vision of a future we'll want to go to. One way to begin painting that future is to reset environmentalism and sustainability — to help them evolve into a larger movement that can touch every part of society. I've tried to offer a version of that future in *The Nature Principle.* I make the case that the future will belong to the nature-smart, the individuals, families, business and political leaders who develop a deeper understanding of the transformative power of the natural world, and who balance the virtual with the real. That's a future worth going to, but first, we have to imagine it.

The barriers between people and nature remain challenging. But we're seeing some change. In the U.S. we're beginning to see progress among state legislatures, schools and businesses, civic organizations, and government agencies. Family nature clubs (multiple families that agree to show up for a hike on Saturday) are proliferating. Regional campaigns are bringing people from across political, religious and economic divides, to connect children to nature. In September 2012, the World Congress of the International Union for the Conservation of Nature (IUCN) cited "adverse consequences for both healthy child development ('nature deficit disorder') as well as responsible stewardship for nature and the environment in the future," and then passed a resolution titled "The Child's Right to Connect with Nature and to a Healthy Environment." This connection is, indeed, a human right. And the acknowledgement of that is progress. While we're seeing progress, many barriers between children and nature still exist, and some are growing. We need leadership at every level and in every country.

I'm inspired by the enthusiastic young people I've met recently and remain hopeful that true cultural change is on the way.

CHILDRENANDNATURE.ORG

Ian McCallum

Co-founder, Cape Town Wilderness Leadership School, South Africa

Ian McCallum is a psychiatrist, poet and wilderness guide and adjunct professor at the Nelson Mandela Metropolitan University Graduate School of Business in Port Elizabeth, South Africa. He is the author of two anthologies of wilderness poems: *Wild Gifts* (1999) and *Untamed* (2012) and a novel, *Thorns to Kilimanjaro* (2000). His award-winning book *Ecological Intelligence — Rediscovering Ourselves in Nature*, addresses the interconnectedness of all living things and ultimately, the survival of the human animal. He is a cofounder of the International League of Conservation Writers, a founding partner of the safari organization Invent Africa, and cofounder of the Cape branch of the Wilderness Leadership School.

How I Stay Inspired

THE CONSERVATION OF WILD areas and wild life protection at whatever level of individual involvement is, I believe, one of the greatest challenges we face as human beings. To me, these precious areas of wildness and the animals that inhabit them, shape them, and in turn, are shaped by them are an essential part of human identity. Who and what would we be without wild life and wild areas in our lives? When they are gone, something deep in us dies with them. When I think of the madness of what is happening to our elephants and rhino, to the large and to the small, I have no option but to regard this great challenge as nothing short of a fight for human sanity. Let us not be fooled; the terrible triad of criminality, financial opportunism and massive indifference to the existence of wild animals is a cancer.

My inspiration to carry on in the work I am doing comes from two sources: from without and within. I am inspired by the incredible work and commitment of the likes of Goodall, Leakey, Sheldrick, Douglas-Hamilton, the late Ian Player and more ... the countless unsung champions of the wild. I salute them. From within, I am inspired by a voice, a deep poetic instinct, a voice that knows without having been taught or advised, that all living things are connected, that we are the human animal. What a privilege. What a responsibility. I have no choice but to be a voice, however significant or small, for the voiceless, for the silenced, and for that which has been silenced in us.

IAN-MCCALLUM.CO.ZA

Todd
Wilkinson

Author, USA

Todd Wilkinson began his career with the legendary City News Bureau of Chicago as a violent crime reporter and he's spent the last 30 years writing about the environment while based in the American West. A contributor to *National Geographic*, the *Christian Science Monitor* and other publications, he is the author most recently of *Grizzlies of Pilgrim Creek, An Intimate Portrait of 399, the Most Famous Bear of Greater Yellowstone*, featuring photographs by Thomas D. Mangelsen, and *Last Stand: Ted Turner's Quest to Save a Troubled Planet*.

How I Stay Inspired

WHEN I'M FEELING DOWN, I unplug myself completely from all gadgetry, head outside to find a peaceful place with a good view, and I write a letter to the future *in longhand*. More specifically, I pen a note to my kids 50 years ahead, knowing that I'll be gone when and if they ever read it. It gives me comfort and solace, solidifying our bond across time and space.

I remind them of the profound joy I've known in nature, sharing their company, the gift we've been given by having other creatures as our neighbors. They are counting on us, I say, to be their voice and advocates; that I know my kids will be the difference they need—because I have complete faith in them, and I've never stopped being inspired by their passion.

We can't afford to go negative, ever. Negativity is the springboard for apathy, sadness, doubt and cynicism. Nothing positive ever came from being dour. Put a message in a biodegradable vessel — no plastic please — and float it to the future.

Tell the recipient you might never know why fighting the good fight feels good, why it matters. And always, always, have a smile on your face while you do it.

I guarantee it will lift you up.

TODDWILKINSONWRITER.COM

Paul
Hilton

Paul Hilton Photography, Hong Kong

In 2009, Paul Hilton became a fellow of the prestigious International League of Conservation Photographers. Presently, based in Hong Kong, he is working on the palm oil issue, documenting deforestation, land clearing, and the wildlife trade in Sumatra's Leuser Ecosystem, Indonesia, in calibration with Rainforest Action Network (RAN), Wildlife Asia and Forest Nature and Environment Aceh (HAkA). Previously, Hilton followed the shark fin and manta and mobula ray trade and set up the Manta Ray of Hope project. Working alongside Wild Aid, Human Society International (HSI), Oceanic Preservation Society (OPS), Greenpeace and Wildlife Conservation Society (WCS), his work has taken him across the world. His undercover footage of the illegal wildlife trade features heavily throughout the 2015 film, *Racing Extinction*.

How I Stay Inspired

"In the midst of winter, I found there was, within me, an invincible summer. And that makes me happy. For it says that no matter how hard the world pushes against me, within me, there's something stronger — something better, pushing right back."

— *Albert Camus*

FIRST AND FOREMOST, the planet is filled with mystery and magic and endless beauty; knowing there are still wild places where intact forests meet oceans teaming with life, keeps me inspired.

Even though I'm confronted with some very depressing scenes of environmental destruction on a weekly basis, from overfishing, deforestation and wildlife crimes, I always return to a place of solitude and reflection within myself and remain very hopeful. This is achieved by a series of exercises in which I write about my experiences; this helps me process what I've witnessed, almost like a kind of download, so as not to hold onto the issue so close but to keep it front and center at the same time. I stay balanced through my own yoga practice and spend time in nature, either surfing or camping. I'm lucky to have a very supportive family and great friends around.

The small victories I've been part of have helped me realize that a small group of people can really change the world. All of us have the power to make change with the choices we make on a daily basis as consumers by demanding that retailers source sustainable products with transparent supply chains.

PAULHILTONPHOTOGRAPHY.COM

Marc Bekoff

Co-founder, Ethologists for the Ethical Treatment of Animals, USA

Marc Bekoff, PhD, is a former professor of ecology and evolutionary biology at the University of Colorado, Boulder, and co-founder with Jane Goodall of Ethologists for the Ethical Treatment of Animals. He has won many awards for his scientific research including the Exemplar Award from the Animal Behavior Society and a Guggenheim Fellowship. In 2009 the New Zealand SPCA presented him with the St. Francis of Assisi Award. Bekoff has published more than 1000 essays and 30 books, including his latest — *Rewilding Our Hearts: Building Pathways of Compassion and Coexistence* and *The Jane Effect: Celebrating Jane Goodall* (edited with Dale Peterson).

Peter Allison

Author, South Africa

Australian born Peter Allison has been a safari guide since 1994, with breaks for occasional exploration outside of Africa. He has written two books about his experiences as a guide, *Whatever You Do, Don't Run;* and *Don't Look Behind You,* as well as stories from his misadventures in searching for jaguars in South America titled *How To Walk A Puma.* He currently lives outside Cape Town with his wife and an immense dog named Mombo.

How I Stay Inspired

CONSERVATION CAN FEEL LIKE windmill tilting, as only bad news gets reported, but on the ground you meet so many people doing such great work and having success. It is mainly small scale, by which I mean the focus is on a single species or single region. None of us can save the entire world, but starting with your own backyard gets you part of the way there.

The tireless work of others, particularly with crises like the rhino-poaching epidemic, stops me from throwing my hands in the air, sitting down and getting drunk until it is all over. Instead, I do what I can to join in, using ecotourism as a way to educate the masses about why some of my favorite places and the animals within them are worth saving.

PETERALLISON.COM

Bill
Wallauer

Videographer, Jane Goodall Institute, USA

Bill Wallauer works for the Jane Goodall Institute and for nearly two decades has scrambled up and down the hills and valleys of Gombe National Park in Tanzania, camera in hand, filming the daily dramas of the world's most famous chimpanzee society. He has served as camera operator and scientific advisor for BBC/Animal Planet, BBC/Discovery *Earth* and as a lead camera and consultant for Disney Nature's movie *Chimpanzee*.

How I Stay Inspired

꩜

DURING MY TRAVELS TO shoot wildlife films or give talks about chimps and chimp conservation, I am often asked the question "How is it possible to remain positive when there is so much 'bad' going on in the world?" True, if you turn on the headline news and listen for a few minutes, you will hear terrible stories of war, tragedy, and destruction being reported day after day, week after week, and it does seem overwhelming. You find yourself asking, what is the point, what difference can I make? To me, *that* is the point. I turn the question on it's head and say: With so many amazing people I hear about and meet, so many truly inspiring leaders and activists, who are working every day to make the world a better place, how can one not feel positive? It is important to keep in perspective that for every story of sadness and violence that comes across the news wire, there are thousands of untold stories that are inspiring and positive. Shocking news sells, so that is what we are fed, but the truth is, there is far more good going on in our communities and around the world than there is "bad."

Yes, there is terrible poverty, gun violence in our streets, war overseas; and I don't want to gloss over that. In some cases it is going to get worse before it gets better, and that is truly depressing. But in every one of our cities, in every community, in every threatened wildlife area, there are phenomenal individuals and groups of amazing people working for change; and that is truly inspiring. Without doubt, the best way to overcome the overwhelming feeling that everything is falling apart, is to join a group of determined people who are working to do good, and you will get swept away in their enthusiasm and power. Look for the great stories of people who have changed policy, cleaned up their neighborhoods, saved a species from extinction, and you will find that thousands of people like you are out there making a difference. Join them!

Jane Goodall is a shining example of what one person can do to make a difference. Her mantra is just that; every one of us matter, every one of us can make a difference every day to make the world a better place for people, animals and the environment. The power we all have together to that end is my true hope and reason for feeling positive. There is a lot of work to be done, but we are on the right track, and I find peace in that thought.

BWALLAUER@JANEGOODALL.ORG

Paul
Johnsgard

Foundation Professor, University Of Nebraska, USA

Paul A. Johnsgard is Foundation Professor of Biological Sciences Emeritus at the University of Nebraska. He has written over 70 scholarly books, including nine world monographs and 250 technical or popular articles, making him the world's most prolific author of ornithological literature. Johnsgard is also a photographer and has illustrated his writings with hundreds of his photos and drawings.

How I Stay Inspired

THE ANSWER FOR ME is simply the infinite variety and complexity of nature. As I walked out of my door this morning I almost stepped into a spider web. I saw it, and a beautiful garden spider, just in time, and stopped a few minutes to admire both the spider and its amazingly intricate web.

Yesterday I watched a family of Baltimore orioles sipping sugar water from a hummingbird feeder in anticipation of their imminent migration, and I wondered where in Central or South America they might be in a month.

It is easy to find inspiration and be awestruck with wonderment; it is usually not far away from one's face, ears, and imagination.

DIGITALCOMMONS.UNL.EDU/BIOSCIORNITHOLOGY/82/

Patricio Robles Gil

Founder, The Human Blue Whale, Mexico

Twenty-five years ago Patricio Robles Gil founded the conservation organizations Sierra Madre and Unidos para la Conservación, both of which he shut down last year. In the early 1990's in Mexico, he pioneered the idea of involving corporations in the protection of wild nature and worked to reintroduce pronghorn and desert bighorn sheep into Coahuila, from where they had disappeared about 70 years ago. In 2009 he helped bring the 9th World Wilderness Congress to Mérida, Yucatan. Patricio has published 38 art books on biodiversity conservation and wilderness. His most recent, *The Onças Pintadas of the Cuiaba River*, is a photographic retelling of 184 encounters with 40 jaguars in the Brazilian Pantanal. He's currently working on *The Rituals of Extinction*, which through art, presents some of the threats imperiling wild nature.

How I Stay Inspired

SOLITUDE IS A STRONG WORD, but it describes my feelings when I'm deep inside an ecosystem with no human footprint. When I spend time in such an environment, I can understand the meaning of certitude, and it is there that my mind finds peace. Creativity, in contrast, a more dynamic word, refers to an ability we humans can play with, in the process striking a bargain with our demons as to the meaning and purpose of our lives. This is why wild nature and art are the two pillars of my world.

It took me a long time to realize that the victories gained in the conservation of nature are fleeting because economic interests will always win in the end . . . it is just a matter of time. No less frustrating was the realization that I don't have the stomach to deal with the betrayals, the greed and the egos of colleagues and partners from other conservation organizations, governments and corporations. With deep sorrow I know now that the wild nature I have cherished so greatly will, in the near future, disappear.

At this point in my life, I'm searching for new ways of expressing myself. My creativity has never been so wide-awake . . . it's as if my demons, those that for so many years were kept silent by the beauty of nature, have surfaced, in the process harassing me on different fronts, with the awareness of the threats to the environment or the problems wild nature faces every day. In this new scenario, I have long conversations with other demons, spirits that inspired the minds of some of the greatest creators in the history of art, and although I have now found a new purpose, it is a much sadder one, to show the destruction of nature.

THEHUMANBLUEWHALE.COM

Tina
Welling

Author, USA

Tina Welling is the author of *Writing Wild, Forming a Creative Partnership with Nature*, published by New World Library. Her three novels are published by the Penguin Group: *Crybaby Ranch, Fairy Tale Blues,* and *Cowboys Never Cry.* Welling's essays have been published in *Shambhala Sun, The Writer, Body & Soul,* and other national magazines, as well as four anthologies. She conducts creative writing and journal keeping workshops around the country, is a public speaker and a long time faculty member of the Jackson Hole Writers Conference.

How I Stay Inspired

WE ARE AMAZING BEINGS. We can accomplish anything we give our attention to. And, to me, that's the key piece: attention. We need to offer our loving minds and hearts to the care of our planet. Once alerted to this need, I believe we'll follow through and we will heal the earth.

I don't see this as an issue of "getting back on track" since we have never historically been on the track of giving to the earth, but rather were always taking. As a species, we have never before faced the realization that in order to live in a way that maintains balance and health, we need to give to the earth and the earth needs to receive from us, just as much as the earth must give to us and we must receive from her.

I feel full of positive energy when I consider the new demands that are required of us. I know we are people who can measure up to this reciprocal exchange between the earth and its inhabitants. And really, we are not discussing two opposing forces here; we are all entwined in this together. So that even the most self-involved of us will find it to be in our best interests to acknowledge the reality of the earth being a live being, one that needs nourishment as much as it needs — in order to be whole — to give nourishment. It's the way all living systems work — plants, animals, the elements, humans, compost, on and on.

Of course, I can become demoralized on occasion. There seems at times to be such an overwhelming need for healing and such an immense denial of it. But life is long, the earth is patient, and once awareness arises it has a way of casting its light far and wide. Astonishing hearts and minds are quietly at work on this issue. All each of us need to do is vow to assist our beautiful planet in the many ways, small and large, that occur to us during our days. It all matters. And, most importantly: Give our attention, our loving, mindful attention to life in all its forms.

TINAWELLING.COM

ACKNOWLEDGMENT

I OWE HEARTFELT THANKS to each of the fifty conservationists for participating in this book. I am in awe of the contributions you make on a daily basis to saving wildlife and wild places and making this a better world. A zillion thanks go to Jane Goodall, who despite her insane schedule, took the time to write what would become the foreword. I can't thank you enough.

My original plan for this book was to do a self-published e-book. Simple enough I thought. How wrong I was. As I read the answers from the conservationists I was so touched and inspired that I began to have bigger dreams for getting this book out into the world. That is when creative director Susan Shankin came into the picture. Thank you, thank you Susan for taking my (once little) project to its highest potential.

Although it is technically correct to list me as the editor, it would be more accurate to say that I conceived of, and then compiled, the book. I have Kate Haas to thank for editing the manuscript.

Thank you Josée Scanlan for your invaluable insight on almost every aspect of the book. Your support and friendship mean the world to me.

I want to also thank Mary Lewis, Melissa White, Suzette Curtis, Tom Burt, Bridget Lewin, Amber Reedy, Janey Cohen, Cam Steele, Madi Vorva, Angie Bell, Lisa Sands, Gary Denny, Connie Speight, Diane Boss, Linda Conger, Joanne Luongo, Janie Chodosh, and all the devoted followers of my blog SavingWild.com.

ABOUT THE AUTHOR

LORI ROBINSON holds degrees in environmental studies, biology and psychology, and has a life-long passion for wildlife and wild places. She has spent time with the indigenous Achuar of the Ecuador Amazon, the Bushmen of the Kalahari Desert, and the Maasai and Samburu of Kenya. From 2004-2010 she worked for the Jane Goodall Institute as their Africa Adventures Specialist and continues to design, and sometimes lead, safaris for clients to East and Southern Africa. She writes about conservation for various blogs and magazines, including Africa Geographic and her own site, SavingWild.com, and is a fellow of the International League of Conservation Writers. She lives alongside coyote, deer, rabbits, and bear in her small old adobe home in Santa Fe, New Mexico. This is her second book.

SAVINGWILD.COM

If you enjoyed reading this book, please share it with others on Facebook, Twitter and other social media. We'd also appreciate your review of it on Amazon or other book review websites.

54735332R00106

Made in the USA
Charleston, SC
10 April 2016